# ONE OF *TIME* MAGAZINE'S
## TOP 10 GRAPHIC NOVELS OF ALL TIME

"A brutal reboot of one of the **greatest** comic book characters ever created... A major superhero had never felt this real before..."

*TIME*

"Frank Miller's THE DARK KNIGHT RETURNS is quite possibly the **single most read** comic book miniseries in history... and it's definitely one of the most influential."

*FORBES*

"An unusually ambitious and **gripping** crime novel"

*ROLLING STONE*

"One of the **best** Batman stories ever told."

*NPR*

"THE DARK KNIGHT RETURNS became a **publishing sensation** and, along with WATCHMEN, ushered in a new era of ambition in the comic book medium that led directly to the contemporary boom in superhero cinema."

*LOS ANGELES TIMES*

"THE DARK KNIGHT RETURNS, for many people **of my generation**, for many people that followed, from the moment it was published forward, is like *The Catcher in the Rye* of comic books."

**KEVIN SMITH**

# FRANK MILLER
### WRITER & PENCILLER

## KLAUS JANSON
### INKER

## LYNN VARLEY
### COLORIST

## JOHN COSTANZA
### LETTERER

BATMAN CREATED BY **BOB KANE** with **BILL FINGER.**

SUPERMAN CREATED BY **JERRY SIEGEL** & **JOE SHUSTER.**

By special arrangement with the Jerry Siegel family.

# BATMAN THE DARK KNIGHT RETURNS

## 30TH ANNIVERSARY EDITION

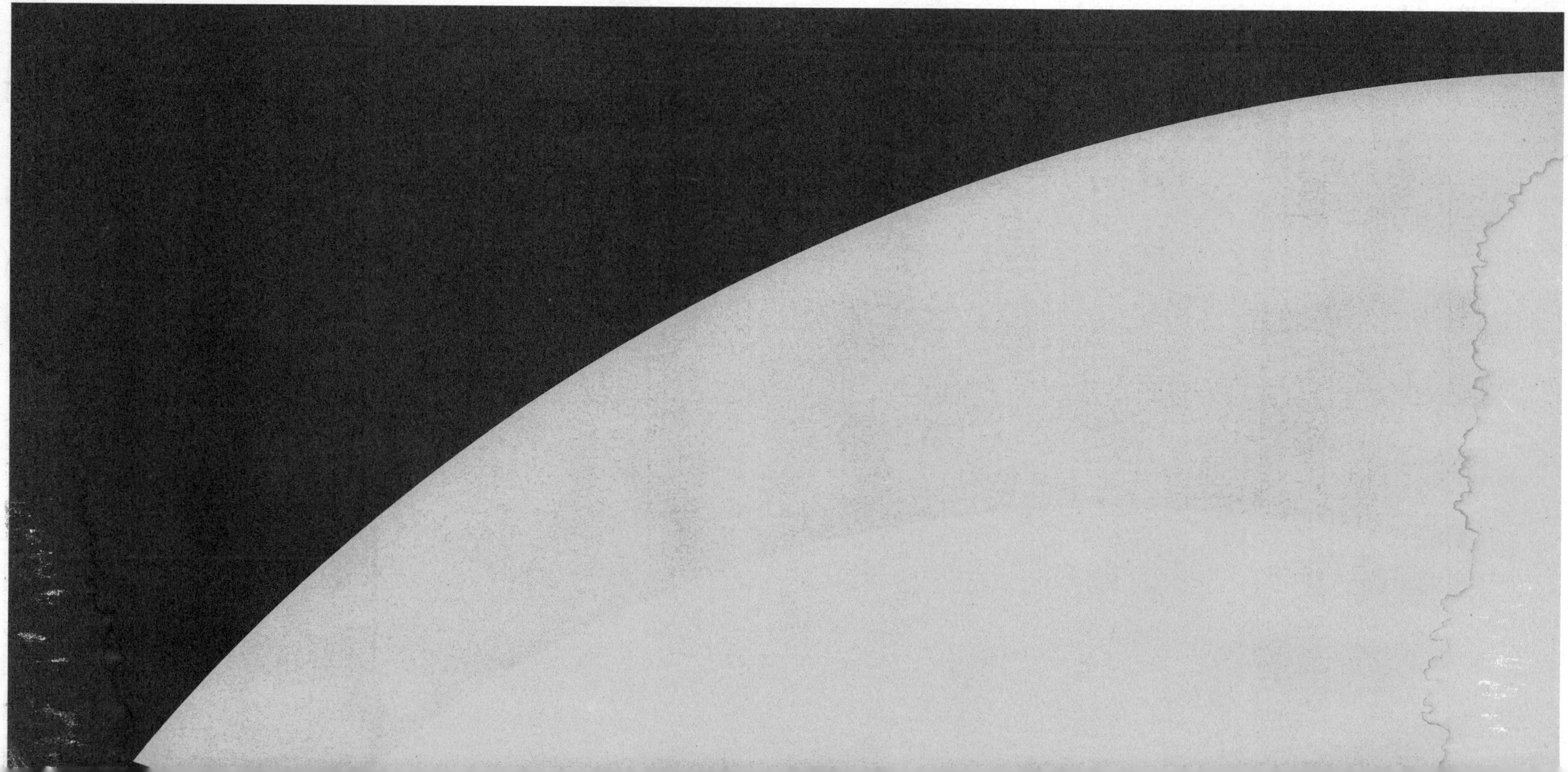

DICK GIORDANO, DENNIS O'NEIL Editors — The Dark Knight Returns, Original Series
JEB WOODARD Group Editor - Collected Editions
STEVE COOK Design Director — Books
DAMIAN RYLAND Publication Design

BOB HARRAS Senior VP — Editor-in-Chief, DC Comics

DIANE NELSON President DAN DIDIO and JIM LEE Co-Publishers GEOFF JOHNS Chief Creative Officer
AMIT DESAI Senior VP — Marketing & Global Franchise Management NAIRI GARDINER Senior VP — Finance
SAM ADES VP — Digital Marketing BOBBIE CHASE VP — Talent Development MARK CHIARELLO Senior VP — Art, Design & Collected Editions
JOHN CUNNINGHAM VP — Content Strategy ANNE DEPIES VP — Strategy Planning & Reporting
DON FALLETTI VP — Manufacturing Operations LAWRENCE GANEM VP — Editorial Administration & Talent Relations
ALISON GILL Senior VP — Manufacturing & Operations HANK KANALZ Senior VP — Editorial Strategy & Administration
JAY KOGAN VP — Legal Affairs DEREK MADDALENA Senior VP — Sales & Business Development
JACK MAHAN VP — Business Affairs DAN MIRON VP — Sales Planning & Trade Development
NICK NAPOLITANO VP — Manufacturing Administration CAROL ROEDER VP — Marketing
EDDIE SCANNELL VP — Mass Account & Digital Sales COURTNEY SIMMONS Senior VP — Publicity & Communications
JIM (SKI) SOKOLOWSKI VP — Comic Book Specialty & Newsstand Sales SANDY YI Senior VP — Global Franchise Management

BATMAN: THE DARK KNIGHT RETURNS 30TH ANNIVERSARY EDITION

With acknowledgements to the works of Bill Finger, Dave Fleischer, Max Fleischer, Jerry Robinson, Joe Shuster, Jerry Siegel and Dick Sprang.

DC Comics, 2900 West Alameda Ave., Burbank, CA 91505.
Printed by RR Donnelley, Salem, VA, USA. 1/8/16. First Printing. ISBN: 978-1-4012-6311-9

Library of Congress Cataloging-in-Publication Data is available.

# IN CAFÉS...

A Conversation between Frank Miller and Brian Azzarello, writers of DARK KNIGHT III: THE MASTER RACE, about BATMAN: THE DARK KNIGHT, its release, and its lasting impact on the world.

**BRIAN:** Let's get in a time machine.

**FRANK:** Okay. No seatbelts, right?

**BRIAN:** Of course not. It's 1986...

**FRANK:** Oh hell, can't we go back farther?

**BRIAN:** Not this time. DARK KNIGHT is about to be released. How do you feel? It's done, it's out of your hands, and now it's gonna go to the stores.

**FRANK:** I am thrilled.

**BRIAN:** I want to know what came first for you, the world or Batman? DARK KNIGHT is so of its time, you know—the whole zeitgeist that was going around in the mid-'80s. Was it, "I want to tell a story with Batman in this world" or "I want to tell a Batman story," and then the world seeped into it?

**FRANK:** No. My intention in the beginning was to tell a story of Batman at the age he would be at this time if he really aged from his origins. He was aged, he was seeing how the world had changed and how he would bring essentially a World War II mentality to the modern world. To him, it wasn't just criminals he was fighting anymore; it was moral decay and political corruption.

**BRIAN:** With DARK KNIGHT in particular, I believe one of your most important contributions to comics is that you brought the real world into superhero comics, where you were using these characters as a way to comment on what was going on all around us at the time in a way no one had ever done before. Prior to DARK KNIGHT, those things were all escapism.

**FRANK:** And Batman was permanently 29, so I decided to make him 50. At 50 I figured he was closer to dead. I made him look like he was at least 60, because that's what I figured 50 would look like. And instead of being lean and muscular, I had him massive. I wanted to bring back the Dick Spring characterization, that rectangular guy.

**BRIAN:** Yeah, he looked like a wrestler or football player when they get older and thick.

**FRANK:** And if you've taken one hit too many. His face is kind of punched in.

**BRIAN:** What was your impetus for doing that the first time?

**FRANK:** Oh, it was very simple: I was 29 years old, I was dreading turning 30. To me that was entering middle age.

**BRIAN:** Were you excited when you started it? Were you trepidatious? I mean, what was your mind-set...this was 30 years ago.

**FRANK:** I remember exactly how I felt—I had been dying to do it for years! The only thing that I knew would be an obstacle was the real reverence for the old stuff. So there was initially fear from DC without realizing that I loved these characters. I had no intention of doing anything obscene.

**BRIAN:** Wasn't necessary.

**FRANK:** I know, it wouldn't serve any purpose.

**BRIAN:** What was Paul [Levitz's] reaction when you brought this story to him, the first one?

**FRANK:** I first brought it to Jenette [Kahn].

**BRIAN:** Before Paul?

**FRANK:** Yeah, and she was thrilled about the idea of the story. We talked to Paul and everybody was completely positive about it. Later, when they actually saw it, they got pretty frightened with the material.

**BRIAN:** Did Jenette ever get frightened?

**FRANK:** No, she was completely supportive, and Paul very swiftly changed his mind when the first issue came out and it went back for a second and third printing.

**BRIAN:** But it created quite a stir. It wasn't instantly the revered tome it is now.

**FRANK:** When it came out, it made many fans very, very angry, but the sales went through the roof, so the dealers were very, very happy. At the same time, the dealers were mostly fans and old collectors who had their comics packed in Mylar snugs. So while I was making them money, I was being accused of violating a trust.

**BRIAN:** You were taking a piss on their childhood.

**FRANK:** To me, I was exulting it.

**BRIAN:** I agree with you, and now 30 years later it's looked at by those very same people you offended as the pinnacle of Batman. I'm not one of those people that look at this work as being so grim and gritty. There's so much political satire in this book.

**FRANK:** I was laughing while I was writing it.

**BRIAN:** I read laughter into a lot of it, too.

**FRANK:** The TV segment with the psychologist, for instance—he would just explain everything, including murder, as being a perfectly healthy function of the human mind.

**BRIAN:** I mean, the book gets a bad wrap for the way that it is dark and gritty, but it's not. I mean, there are moments, certainly, but those moments only work because they're played against some real broad satire. Even the first time we see Superman, he's got birds around and the sky is all beautiful...

**FRANK:** And there's Bruce Wayne all cranky. I figured that Clark would only age in terms of handsome wrinkles around his eyes. Otherwise he'd be as iconic as ever, while Batman was just old.

**BRIAN:** While DK wasn't my introduction to Batman, it definitely was my introduction to Batman as a figure in a comic book. I read it when it was originally coming out, and I was blown away by how you made superhero characters relevant. Really, it was revolutionary. And it was crazy—even the naysayers were on board for the thrill ride. Each issue, you topped yourself.

**FRANK:** I particularly liked doing the cover to the second one, where he was just beat to crap, just because of the idea of him being someone who's kind of like Rocky. He could take punches better than he could throw them. He could take any punishment you gave him and keep coming.

**BRIAN:** Which he did. The second one, that was the mutant issue.

**FRANK:** The guy with the sharp teeth.

**BRIAN:** That was Batman taking a lot of punishment in that one.

**FRANK:** Mr. T was a real popular figure at the time.

**BRIAN:** Clubber Lang.

**FRANK:** And I patterned his speech as close to Mr. T's as I could.

**BRIAN:** Wow.

**FRANK:** I know. I came up with mutant colloquialism from Lynn Varley, who colored DARK KNIGHT. There was a language she and her brothers had amongst themselves that fascinated me, so I had all the mutants speak that way.

**BRIAN:** Where were you living when you wrote that? Were you here? New York? It had a dangerous reputation at the time.

**FRANK:** Oh, it was a very bad time. Koch was mayor and he was doing his best to clean things up. Crime was rampant and I had been mugged a few times. I was very, very angry, just watching Clint Eastwood movies back to back, getting absolutely paranoid. I figured if Batman was a grown-up, he'd take care of things.

**BRIAN:** Was it post- or pre-Bernhard Goetz?

**FRANK:** Goetz did what he did while I was working on the first issue. It was all very coincidental.

**BRIAN:** Like I said, it was something about the zeitgeist and you were definitely plugged into it at the time. You know, Batman's 75th anniversary just passed, and it's been 30 years since DARK KNIGHT was released. Your book and your take on Batman has informed the character for nearly half of his existence.

**FRANK:** Could you order me a wheelchair right now?

**BRIAN:** I'd be happy to. One for Bruce as well.

So, now it's 30 years later. Looking at the impact the book has had, how do you feel about it?

**FRANK:** Something Walter Simonson told me was really valuable, which is that when amateurs want to learn from a professional, the thing they tend to learn most often is the professional's mistakes. And so I saw a lot of my faults as an artist replicated by amateurs, and it taught me a lot about how to communicate better. With all my quirks replicated, I saw really how weak my drawing was, and in many ways I learned to make it better. That's been its impact on me, on comics in general. It did affect how creators have paced stories, and that's good somewhat.

The main thing DARK KNIGHT has done is it's given both writers and artists much more freedom to maneuver, and we've taken these once-precious characters in new directions. DARK KNIGHT has been so successful, publishers have realized they have to publish this kind of stuff without putting a condom on it.

—Paris & New York City, November 2015

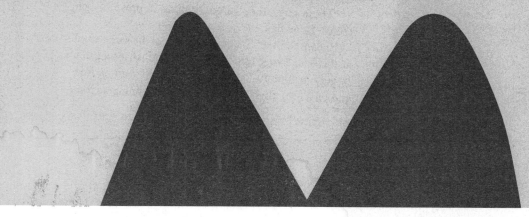

# TRUTH TO POWER

## By JAMES OLSEN

There's this little saloon you'll find up and running and packed with patrons before most of us are ready for our morning coffee.

The joint's two subway levels beneath the streets of downtown Metropolis.

Step out at the Shuster stop on the southbound side, take two lefts, walk maybe fifteen feet and you're right on top of it.

But you could just as easily walk right past it and never know it was there.

There's no sign up. Not even a door. Just a dark hallway that looks like a good place for a murder.

Take a breath. Follow the cigarette stink and the bluesy jukebox sounds inside.

It's a tolerable little gin mill. Get there before the morning rush, and you're likely to find a stool.

Your first clue that there's something wrong about the place is the bartender. You'll never forget his face. He's a hulk of a guy who's seen way too much. A broken man with laser-red eyes. His forehead's a fractured cantilever, an avalanche waiting to happen. His skin's gone a little gray from its natural chartreuse.

He's got a voice like Coke bottles getting ground up under a door.

His name is Jones.

He says he's from Mars.

And nobody tells him he's nuts, not one of these sad old barflies. It's not that they're scared of him, either.

They've seen and done things that are supposed to be impossible.

They're not the kind to out-and-out brag about being able to bench-press cars or run faster than a speeding bullet or jump up into the air and stay there. Nah. Not these guys.

These guys, they've got nothing to prove. Been there. Done that.

Except for old "Snapper" always at the same stool at the end, living up to his nickname, snapping his fingers in time to the music and rattling on and on and on about mighty powers, globe-spanning adven-

*Continued on page A24*

*Continued from page A1*

tures, nefarious world conquerors, you name it.

He never stops snapping his damn fingers. And he never stops sucking back the sauce and jabbering about the old days. The glory days.

The "Golden Age" he calls it.

The age of heroes.

And all the other old farts, they grunt and nod and grumble at each other, swapping old jokes they've swapped a thousand times. Even fat, beet-red old "Penguin" chirps out a curse or two before bursting into tears.

Then they get talking. And if you've got half a brain, you listen.

They talk about amazing adventures, sounding like a bunch of retired car mechanics the whole time.

They talk about a Man of Steel. An Amazon Princess.

But they never talk about the mean one. The cruel one. The one who couldn't fly or bend steel in his bare hands. The one who scared the crap out of everybody and laughed at all of the rest of us for being the envious cowards we were.

No, they never talk about him. Say his name and watch Dibny's face sag so bad his jaw hits the bar.

Not a man among them wants to hear about Batman.

Was he quietly assassinated? Or did he just decide we weren't worth the grief?

The question hangs in the air for a moment or two, then Jones springs for a round for everybody and himself.

They get talking again. About the old days. The glory days.

They remember.

They were right there. In the thick of it.

Back then.

It wasn't so long ago.

We had heroes.

The Daily Planet

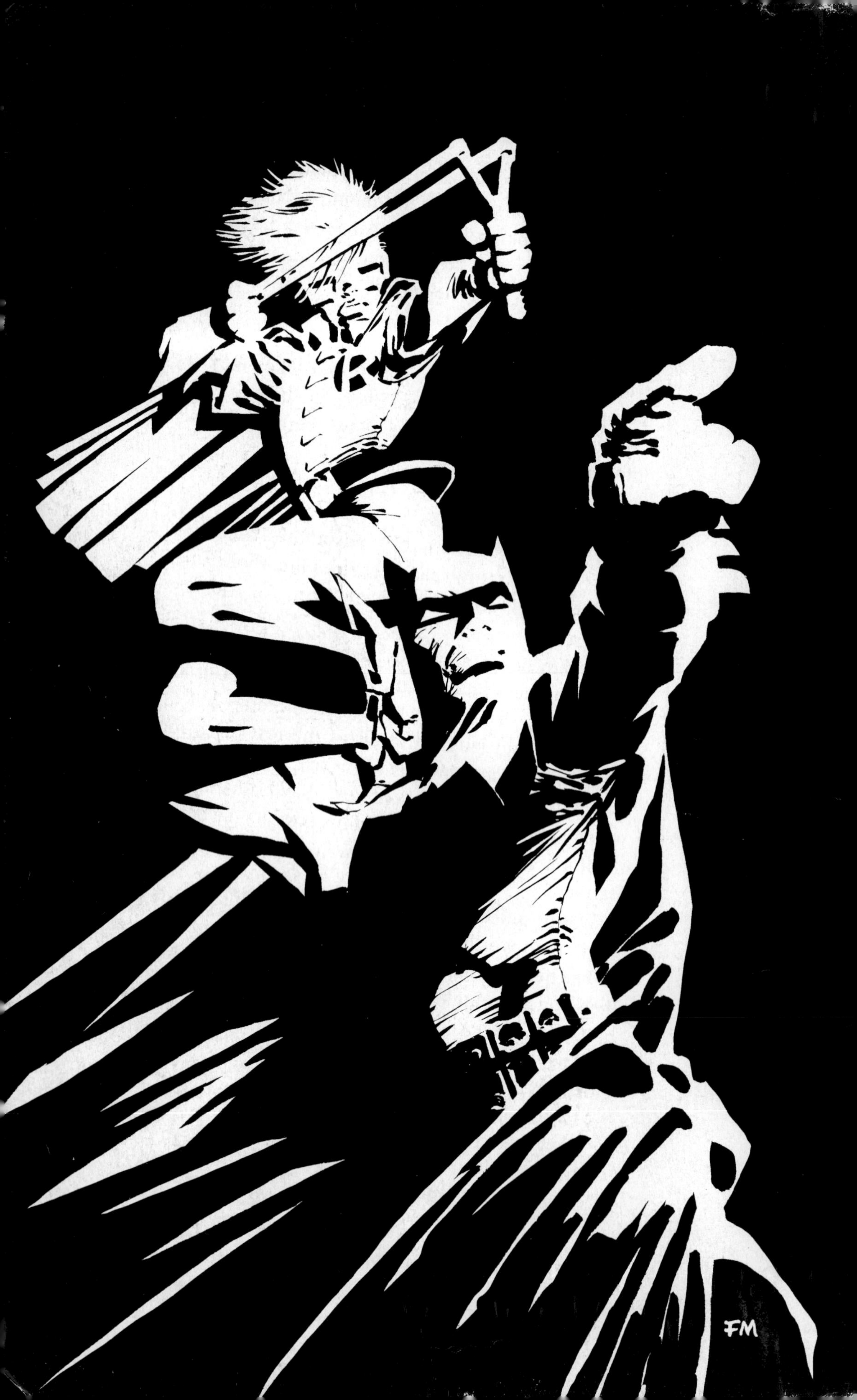
FM

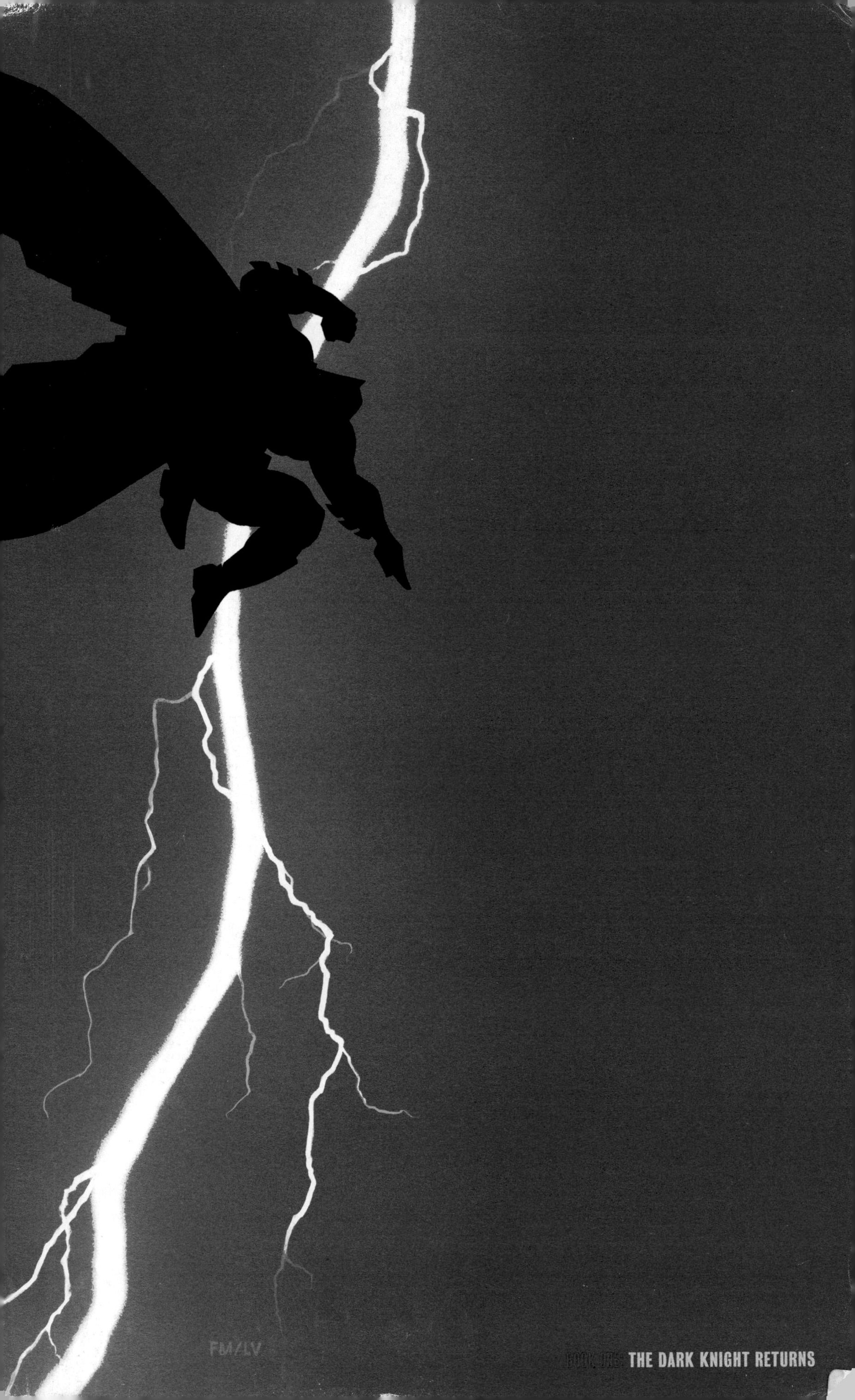
FM/LV
BOOK ONE THE DARK KNIGHT RETURNS

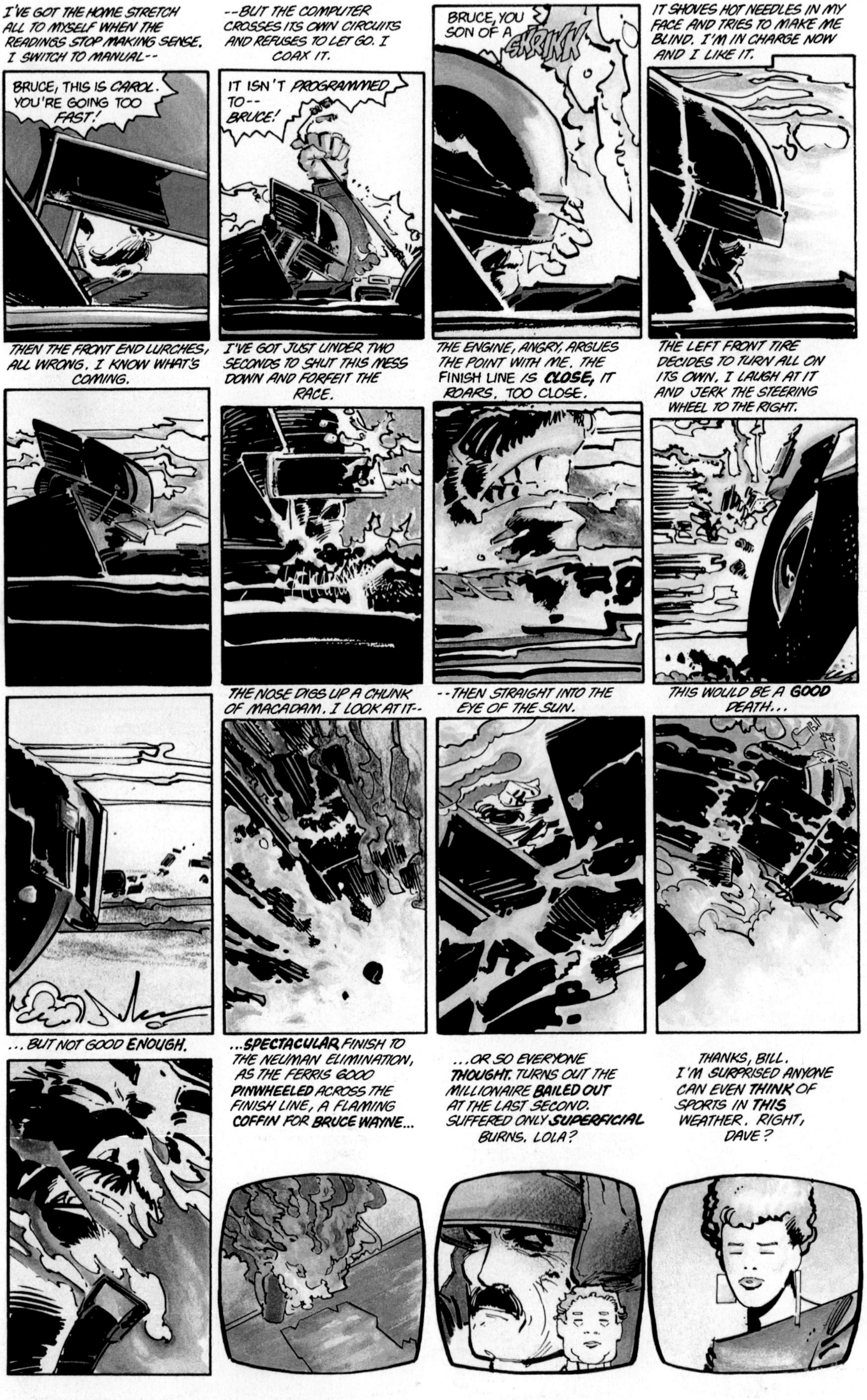
I'VE GOT THE HOME STRETCH ALL TO MYSELF WHEN THE READINGS STOP MAKING SENSE. I SWITCH TO MANUAL--
BRUCE, THIS IS CAROL. YOU'RE GOING TOO FAST!
--BUT THE COMPUTER CROSSES ITS OWN CIRCUITS AND REFUSES TO LET GO. I COAX IT.
IT ISN'T PROGRAMMED TO-- BRUCE!
BRUCE, YOU SON OF A
SKRINK
IT SHOVES HOT NEEDLES IN MY FACE AND TRIES TO MAKE ME BLIND. I'M IN CHARGE NOW AND I LIKE IT.
THEN THE FRONT END LURCHES, ALL WRONG. I KNOW WHAT'S COMING.
I'VE GOT JUST UNDER TWO SECONDS TO SHUT THIS MESS DOWN AND FORFEIT THE RACE.
THE ENGINE, ANGRY, ARGUES THE POINT WITH ME. THE FINISH LINE IS CLOSE, IT ROARS. TOO CLOSE.
THE LEFT FRONT TIRE DECIDES TO TURN ALL ON ITS OWN. I LAUGH AT IT AND JERK THE STEERING WHEEL TO THE RIGHT.
THE NOSE DIGS UP A CHUNK OF MACADAM. I LOOK AT IT--
--THEN STRAIGHT INTO THE EYE OF THE SUN.
THIS WOULD BE A GOOD DEATH...
...BUT NOT GOOD ENOUGH.
...SPECTACULAR FINISH TO THE NEUMAN ELIMINATION, AS THE FERRIS 6000 PINWHEELED ACROSS THE FINISH LINE, A FLAMING COFFIN FOR BRUCE WAYNE...
...OR SO EVERYONE THOUGHT. TURNS OUT THE MILLIONAIRE BAILED OUT AT THE LAST SECOND. SUFFERED ONLY SUPERFICIAL BURNS. LOLA?
THANKS, BILL. I'M SURPRISED ANYONE CAN EVEN THINK OF SPORTS IN THIS WEATHER. RIGHT, DAVE?

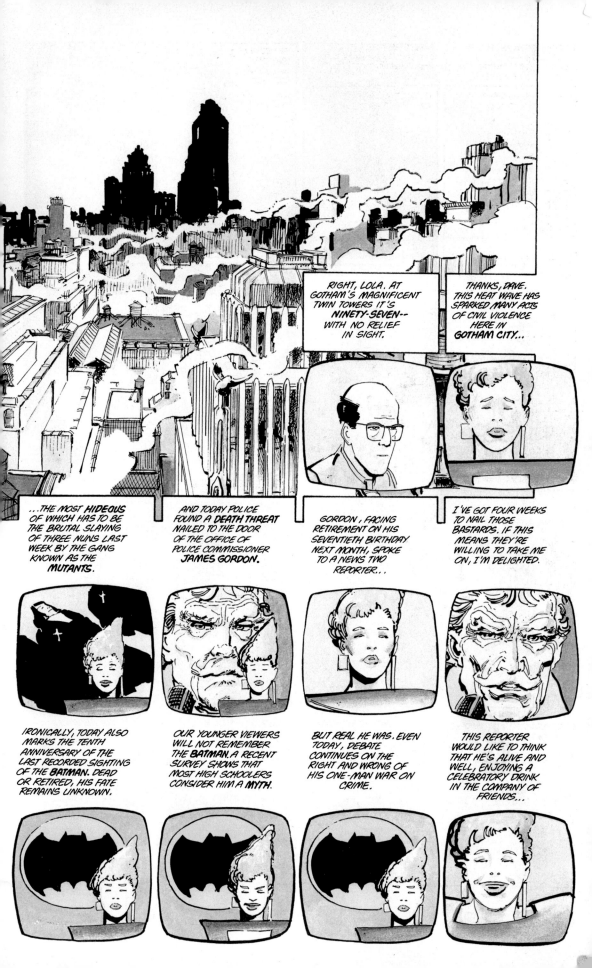

RIGHT, LOLA. AT GOTHAM'S MAGNIFICENT TWIN TOWERS IT'S **NINETY-SEVEN**-- WITH NO RELIEF IN SIGHT.

THANKS, DAVE. THIS HEAT WAVE HAS SPARKED MANY ACTS OF CIVIL VIOLENCE HERE IN **GOTHAM CITY**...

...THE MOST **HIDEOUS** OF WHICH HAS TO BE THE BRUTAL SLAYING OF THREE NUNS LAST WEEK BY THE GANG KNOWN AS THE **MUTANTS**.

AND TODAY POLICE FOUND A **DEATH THREAT** NAILED TO THE DOOR OF THE OFFICE OF POLICE COMMISSIONER **JAMES GORDON**.

GORDON, FACING RETIREMENT ON HIS SEVENTIETH BIRTHDAY NEXT MONTH, SPOKE TO A NEWS TWO REPORTER...

I'VE GOT FOUR WEEKS TO NAIL THOSE BASTARDS. IF THIS MEANS THEY'RE WILLING TO TAKE ME ON, I'M DELIGHTED.

IRONICALLY, TODAY ALSO MARKS THE TENTH ANNIVERSARY OF THE LAST RECORDED SIGHTING OF THE **BATMAN**. DEAD OR RETIRED, HIS FATE REMAINS UNKNOWN.

OUR YOUNGER VIEWERS WILL NOT REMEMBER THE **BATMAN**. A RECENT SURVEY SHOWS THAT MOST HIGH SCHOOLERS CONSIDER HIM A **MYTH**.

BUT REAL HE WAS. EVEN TODAY, DEBATE CONTINUES ON THE RIGHT AND WRONG OF HIS ONE-MAN WAR ON CRIME.

THIS REPORTER WOULD LIKE TO THINK THAT HE'S ALIVE AND WELL, ENJOYING A CELEBRATORY DRINK IN THE COMPANY OF FRIENDS...

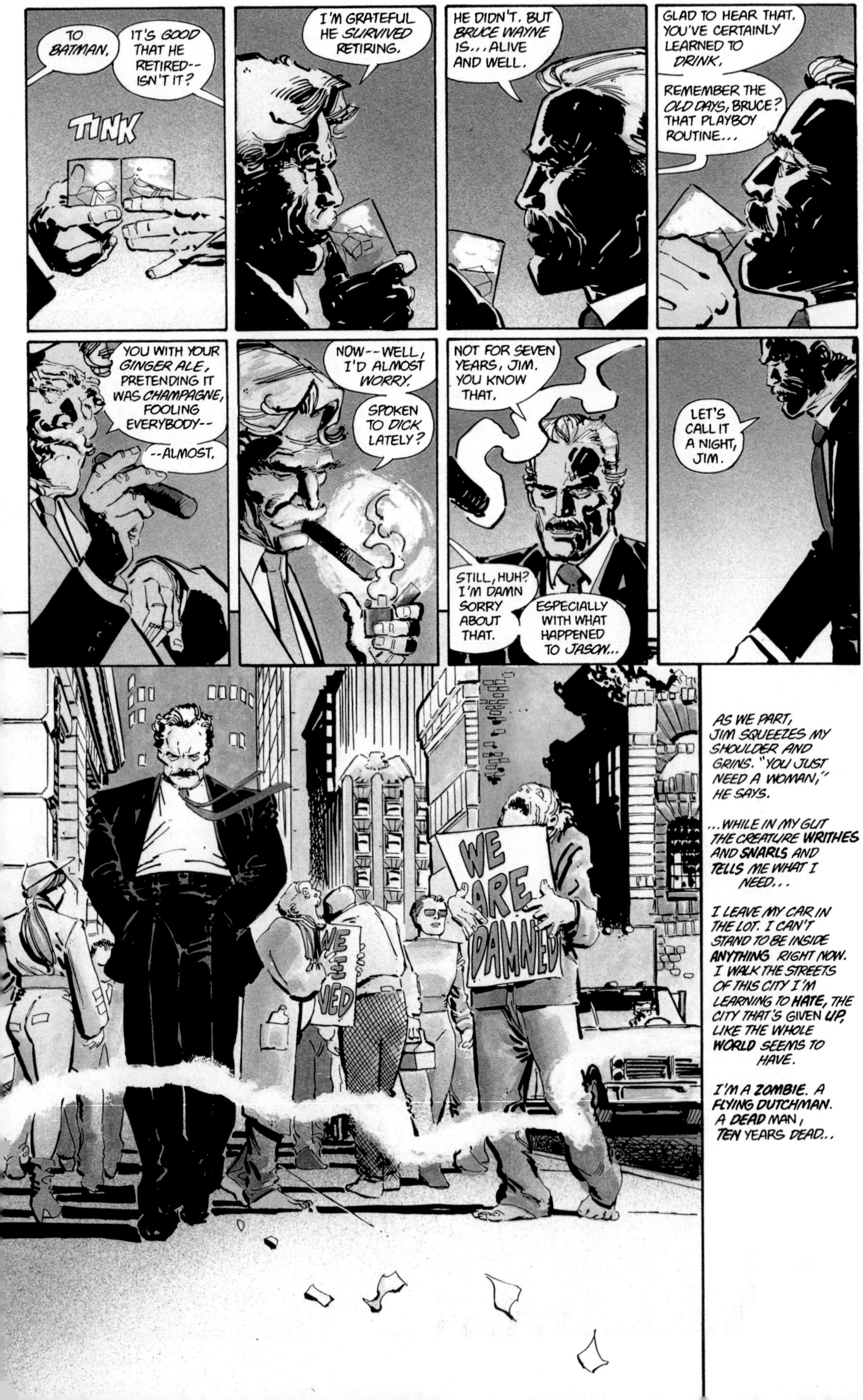
TO BATMAN.
IT'S GOOD THAT HE RETIRED-- ISN'T IT?
TINK
I'M GRATEFUL HE SURVIVED RETIRING.
HE DIDN'T. BUT BRUCE WAYNE IS... ALIVE AND WELL.
GLAD TO HEAR THAT. YOU'VE CERTAINLY LEARNED TO DRINK.
REMEMBER THE OLD DAYS, BRUCE? THAT PLAYBOY ROUTINE...
YOU WITH YOUR GINGER ALE, PRETENDING IT WAS CHAMPAGNE, FOOLING EVERYBODY--
--ALMOST.
NOW--WELL, I'D ALMOST WORRY.
SPOKEN TO DICK LATELY?
NOT FOR SEVEN YEARS, JIM. YOU KNOW THAT.
STILL, HUH? I'M DAMN SORRY ABOUT THAT.
ESPECIALLY WITH WHAT HAPPENED TO JASON...
LET'S CALL IT A NIGHT, JIM.
WE ARE DAMNED
AS WE PART, JIM SQUEEZES MY SHOULDER AND GRINS. "YOU JUST NEED A WOMAN," HE SAYS.
...WHILE IN MY GUT THE CREATURE WRITHES AND SNARLS AND TELLS ME WHAT I NEED...
I LEAVE MY CAR IN THE LOT. I CAN'T STAND TO BE INSIDE ANYTHING RIGHT NOW. I WALK THE STREETS OF THIS CITY I'M LEARNING TO HATE, THE CITY THAT'S GIVEN UP, LIKE THE WHOLE WORLD SEEMS TO HAVE.
I'M A ZOMBIE. A FLYING DUTCHMAN. A DEAD MAN, TEN YEARS DEAD...

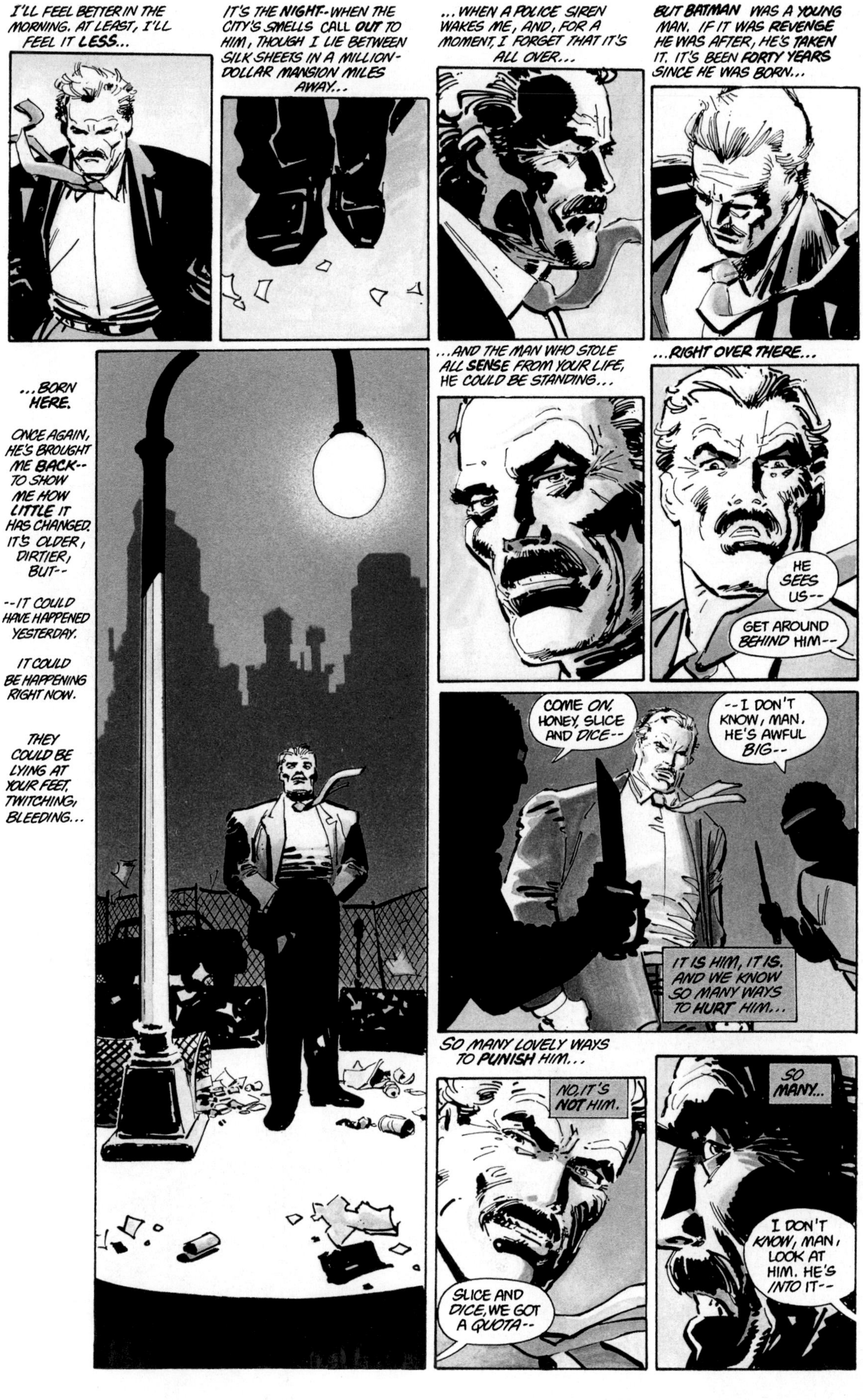
I'LL FEEL BETTER IN THE MORNING. AT LEAST, I'LL FEEL IT LESS...
IT'S THE NIGHT--WHEN THE CITY'S SMELLS CALL OUT TO HIM, THOUGH I LIE BETWEEN SILK SHEETS IN A MILLION-DOLLAR MANSION MILES AWAY...
...WHEN A POLICE SIREN WAKES ME, AND, FOR A MOMENT, I FORGET THAT IT'S ALL OVER...
BUT BATMAN WAS A YOUNG MAN. IF IT WAS REVENGE HE WAS AFTER, HE'S TAKEN IT. IT'S BEEN FORTY YEARS SINCE HE WAS BORN...
...BORN HERE.
ONCE AGAIN, HE'S BROUGHT ME BACK-- TO SHOW ME HOW LITTLE IT HAS CHANGED. IT'S OLDER, DIRTIER, BUT--
--IT COULD HAVE HAPPENED YESTERDAY.
IT COULD BE HAPPENING RIGHT NOW.
THEY COULD BE LYING AT YOUR FEET, TWITCHING, BLEEDING...
...AND THE MAN WHO STOLE ALL SENSE FROM YOUR LIFE, HE COULD BE STANDING...
...RIGHT OVER THERE...
HE SEES US--
GET AROUND BEHIND HIM--
COME ON, HONEY, SLICE AND DICE--
--I DON'T KNOW, MAN. HE'S AWFUL BIG--
IT IS HIM, IT IS. AND WE KNOW SO MANY WAYS TO HURT HIM...
SO MANY LOVELY WAYS TO PUNISH HIM...
NO, IT'S NOT HIM.
SLICE AND DICE, WE GOT A QUOTA--
SO MANY...
I DON'T KNOW, MAN, LOOK AT HIM. HE'S INTO IT--

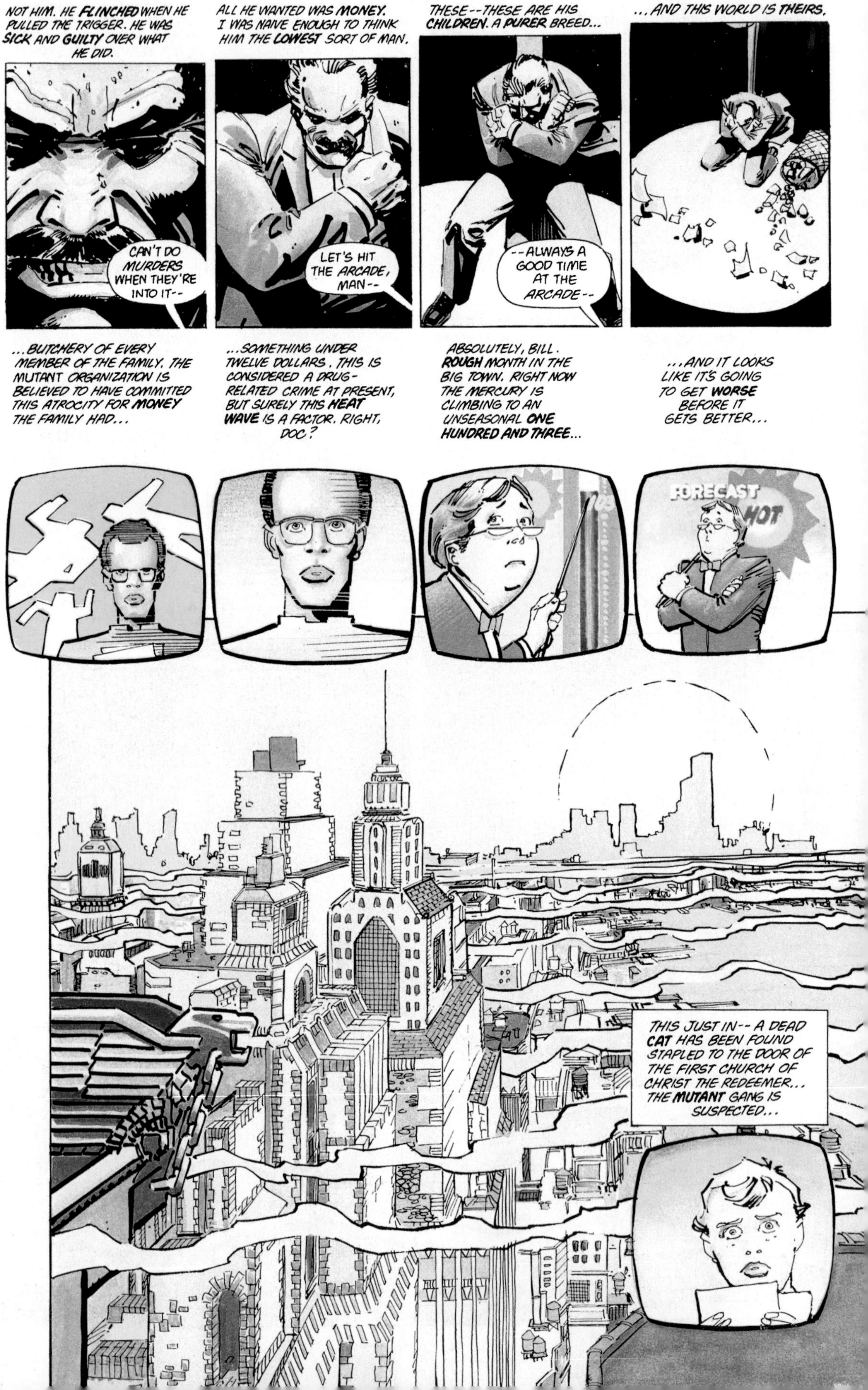

NOT HIM. HE FLINCHED WHEN HE PULLED THE TRIGGER. HE WAS SICK AND GUILTY OVER WHAT HE DID.
CAN'T DO MURDERS WHEN THEY'RE INTO IT--
ALL HE WANTED WAS MONEY. I WAS NAIVE ENOUGH TO THINK HIM THE LOWEST SORT OF MAN.
LET'S HIT THE ARCADE, MAN--
THESE--THESE ARE HIS CHILDREN. A PURER BREED...
--ALWAYS A GOOD TIME AT THE ARCADE--
...AND THIS WORLD IS THEIRS.
...BUTCHERY OF EVERY MEMBER OF THE FAMILY. THE MUTANT ORGANIZATION IS BELIEVED TO HAVE COMMITTED THIS ATROCITY FOR MONEY THE FAMILY HAD...
...SOMETHING UNDER TWELVE DOLLARS. THIS IS CONSIDERED A DRUG-RELATED CRIME AT PRESENT, BUT SURELY THIS HEAT WAVE IS A FACTOR. RIGHT, DOC?
ABSOLUTELY, BILL. ROUGH MONTH IN THE BIG TOWN. RIGHT NOW THE MERCURY IS CLIMBING TO AN UNSEASONAL ONE HUNDRED AND THREE...
...AND IT LOOKS LIKE IT'S GOING TO GET WORSE BEFORE IT GETS BETTER...
FORECAST
HOT
THIS JUST IN-- A DEAD CAT HAS BEEN FOUND STAPLED TO THE DOOR OF THE FIRST CHURCH OF CHRIST THE REDEEMER... THE MUTANT GANG IS SUSPECTED...

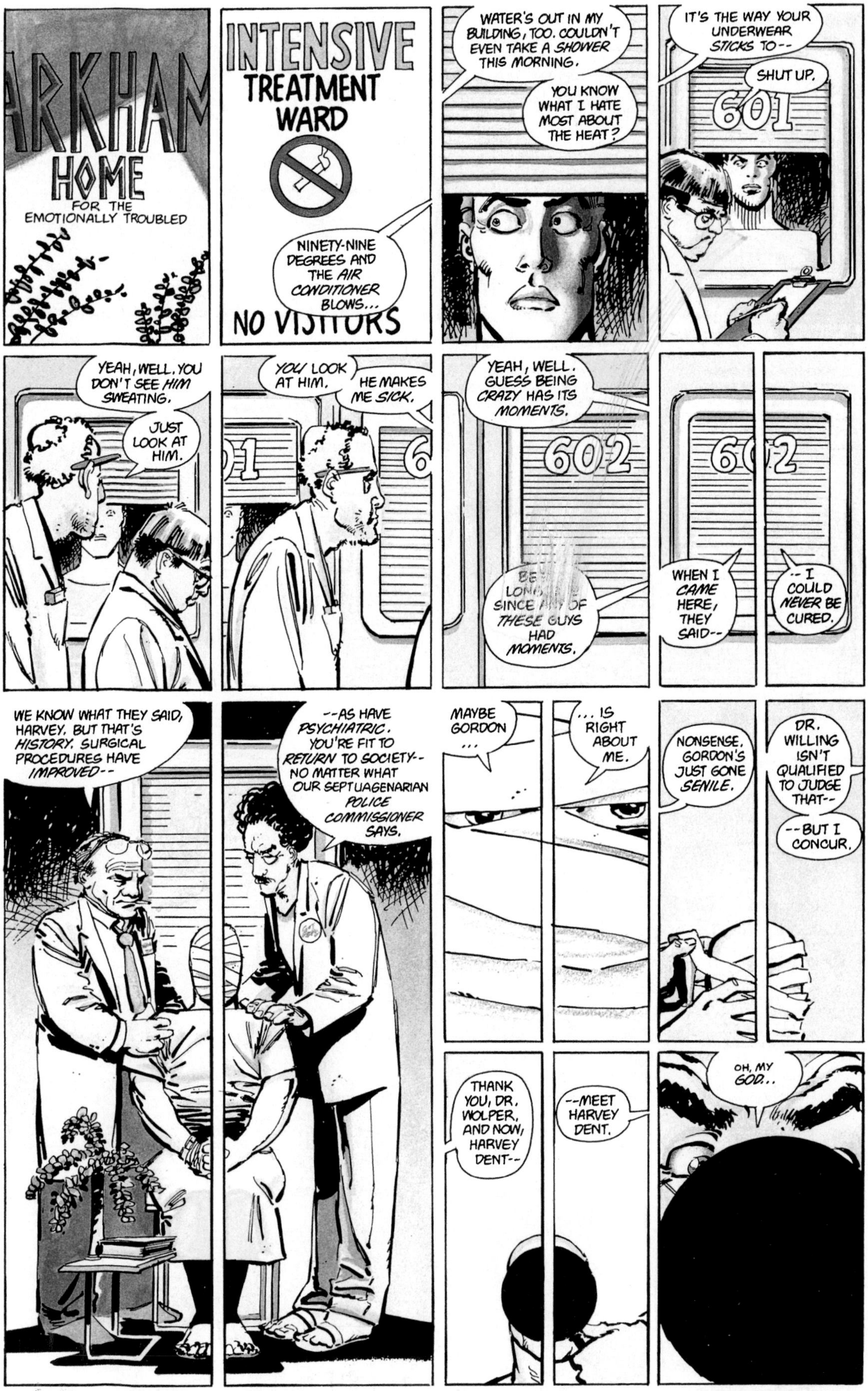
ARKHAM HOME FOR THE EMOTIONALLY TROUBLED
INTENSIVE TREATMENT WARD
NO VISITORS
NINETY-NINE DEGREES AND THE AIR CONDITIONER BLOWS...
WATER'S OUT IN MY BUILDING, TOO. COULDN'T EVEN TAKE A SHOWER THIS MORNING.
YOU KNOW WHAT I HATE MOST ABOUT THE HEAT?
IT'S THE WAY YOUR UNDERWEAR STICKS TO--
SHUT UP.
601
YEAH, WELL, YOU DON'T SEE HIM SWEATING.
JUST LOOK AT HIM.
YOU LOOK AT HIM.
HE MAKES ME SICK.
YEAH, WELL. GUESS BEING CRAZY HAS ITS MOMENTS.
602
THESE GUYS HAD MOMENTS.
WHEN I CAME HERE, THEY SAID--
--I COULD NEVER BE CURED.
WE KNOW WHAT THEY SAID, HARVEY. BUT THAT'S HISTORY. SURGICAL PROCEDURES HAVE IMPROVED--
--AS HAVE PSYCHIATRIC. YOU'RE FIT TO RETURN TO SOCIETY--NO MATTER WHAT OUR SEPTUAGENARIAN POLICE COMMISSIONER SAYS.
MAYBE GORDON ...
... IS RIGHT ABOUT ME.
NONSENSE. GORDON'S JUST GONE SENILE.
DR. WILLING ISN'T QUALIFIED TO JUDGE THAT--
--BUT I CONCUR.
THANK YOU, DR. WOLPER. AND NOW, HARVEY DENT--
--MEET HARVEY DENT.
OH, MY GOD...

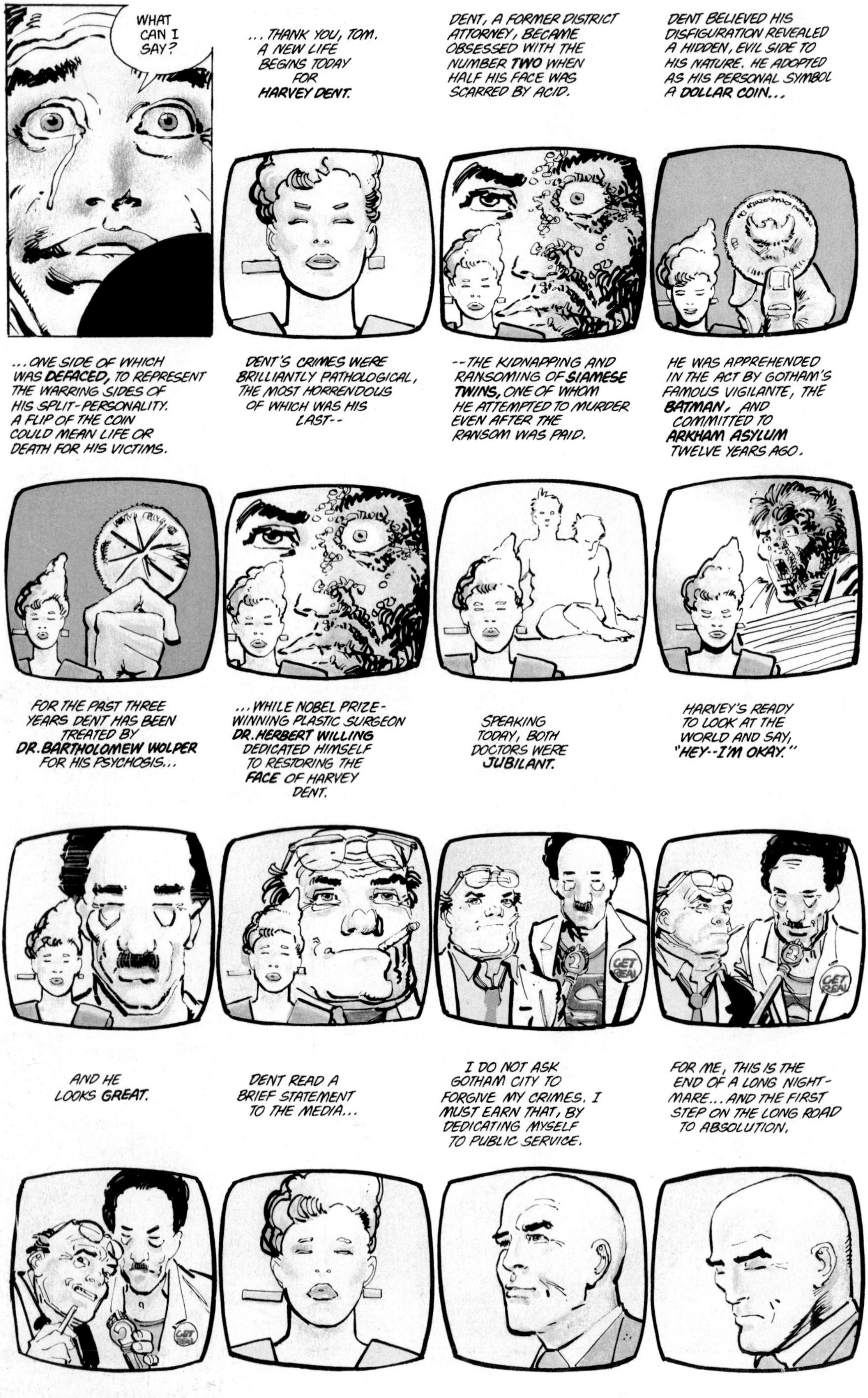
WHAT CAN I SAY?
...THANK YOU, TOM. A NEW LIFE BEGINS TODAY FOR HARVEY DENT.
DENT, A FORMER DISTRICT ATTORNEY, BECAME OBSESSED WITH THE NUMBER TWO WHEN HALF HIS FACE WAS SCARRED BY ACID.
DENT BELIEVED HIS DISFIGURATION REVEALED A HIDDEN, EVIL SIDE TO HIS NATURE. HE ADOPTED AS HIS PERSONAL SYMBOL A DOLLAR COIN...
...ONE SIDE OF WHICH WAS DEFACED, TO REPRESENT THE WARRING SIDES OF HIS SPLIT-PERSONALITY. A FLIP OF THE COIN COULD MEAN LIFE OR DEATH FOR HIS VICTIMS.
DENT'S CRIMES WERE BRILLIANTLY PATHOLOGICAL, THE MOST HORRENDOUS OF WHICH WAS HIS LAST--
--THE KIDNAPPING AND RANSOMING OF SIAMESE TWINS, ONE OF WHOM HE ATTEMPTED TO MURDER EVEN AFTER THE RANSOM WAS PAID.
HE WAS APPREHENDED IN THE ACT BY GOTHAM'S FAMOUS VIGILANTE, THE BATMAN, AND COMMITTED TO ARKHAM ASYLUM TWELVE YEARS AGO.
FOR THE PAST THREE YEARS DENT HAS BEEN TREATED BY DR. BARTHOLOMEW WOLPER FOR HIS PSYCHOSIS...
...WHILE NOBEL PRIZE-WINNING PLASTIC SURGEON DR. HERBERT WILLING DEDICATED HIMSELF TO RESTORING THE FACE OF HARVEY DENT.
SPEAKING TODAY, BOTH DOCTORS WERE JUBILANT.
HARVEY'S READY TO LOOK AT THE WORLD AND SAY, "HEY--I'M OKAY."
GET REAL
GET REAL
AND HE LOOKS GREAT.
DENT READ A BRIEF STATEMENT TO THE MEDIA...
I DO NOT ASK GOTHAM CITY TO FORGIVE MY CRIMES. I MUST EARN THAT, BY DEDICATING MYSELF TO PUBLIC SERVICE.
FOR ME, THIS IS THE END OF A LONG NIGHTMARE... AND THE FIRST STEP ON THE LONG ROAD TO ABSOLUTION.
GET REAL

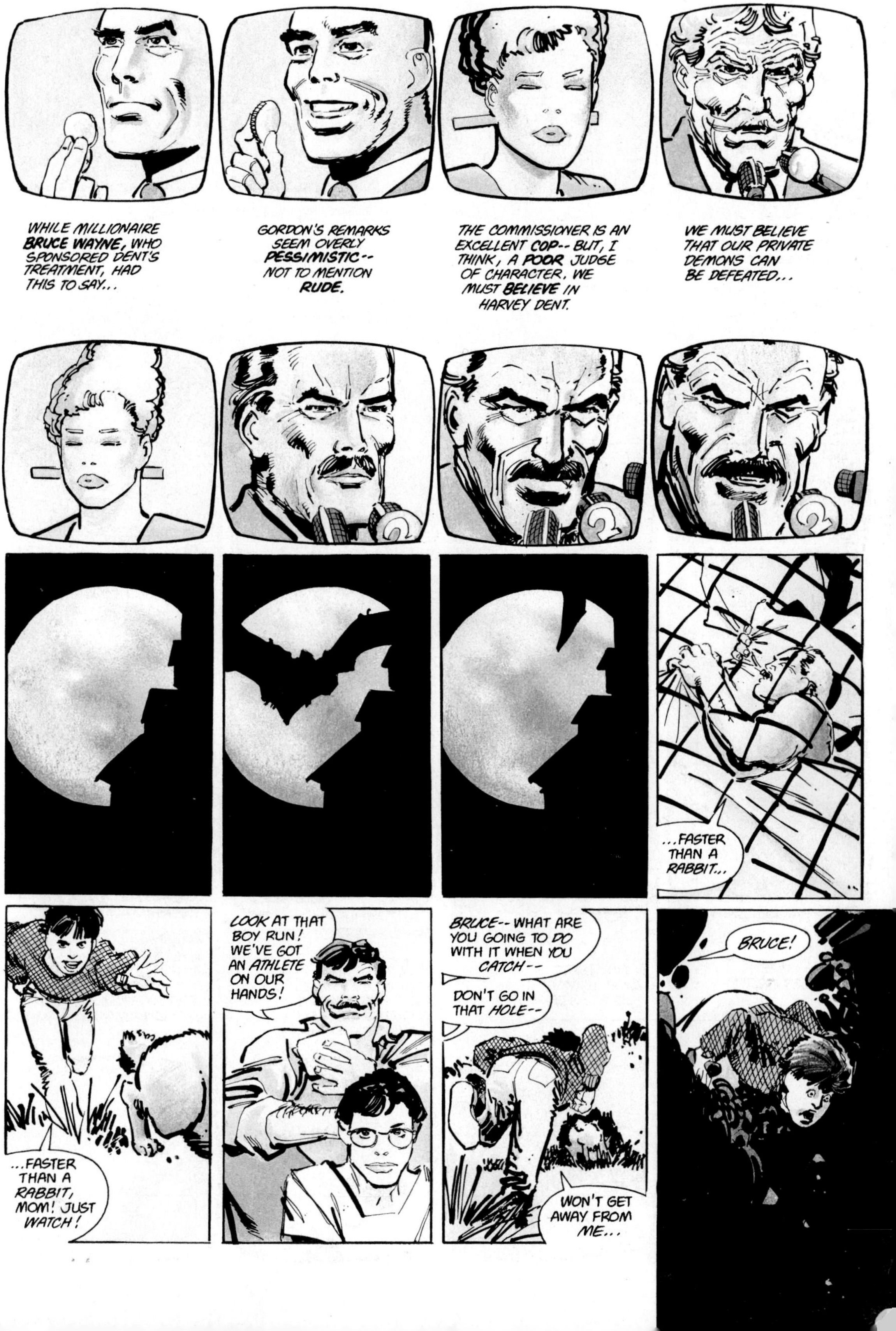
NEXT, DENT DREW FOND APPLAUSE BY PRODUCING A NEWLY-MINTED DOLLAR COIN.
IT WAS, OF COURSE, UNMARRED.
BUT POLICE COMMISSIONER JAMES GORDON'S REACTION TO DENT'S RELEASE WAS NOT ENTHUSIASTIC...
NO, I AM NOT SATISFIED. DR. WOLPER'S REPORT SEEMS OVERLY OPTIMISTIC-- NOT TO MENTION SLOPPY.
WHILE MILLIONAIRE BRUCE WAYNE, WHO SPONSORED DENT'S TREATMENT, HAD THIS TO SAY...
GORDON'S REMARKS SEEM OVERLY PESSIMISTIC-- NOT TO MENTION RUDE.
THE COMMISSIONER IS AN EXCELLENT COP-- BUT, I THINK, A POOR JUDGE OF CHARACTER. WE MUST BELIEVE IN HARVEY DENT.
WE MUST BELIEVE THAT OUR PRIVATE DEMONS CAN BE DEFEATED...
...FASTER THAN A RABBIT...
...FASTER THAN A RABBIT, MOM! JUST WATCH!
LOOK AT THAT BOY RUN! WE'VE GOT AN ATHLETE ON OUR HANDS!
BRUCE-- WHAT ARE YOU GOING TO DO WITH IT WHEN YOU CATCH--
DON'T GO IN THAT HOLE--
WON'T GET AWAY FROM ME...
BRUCE!

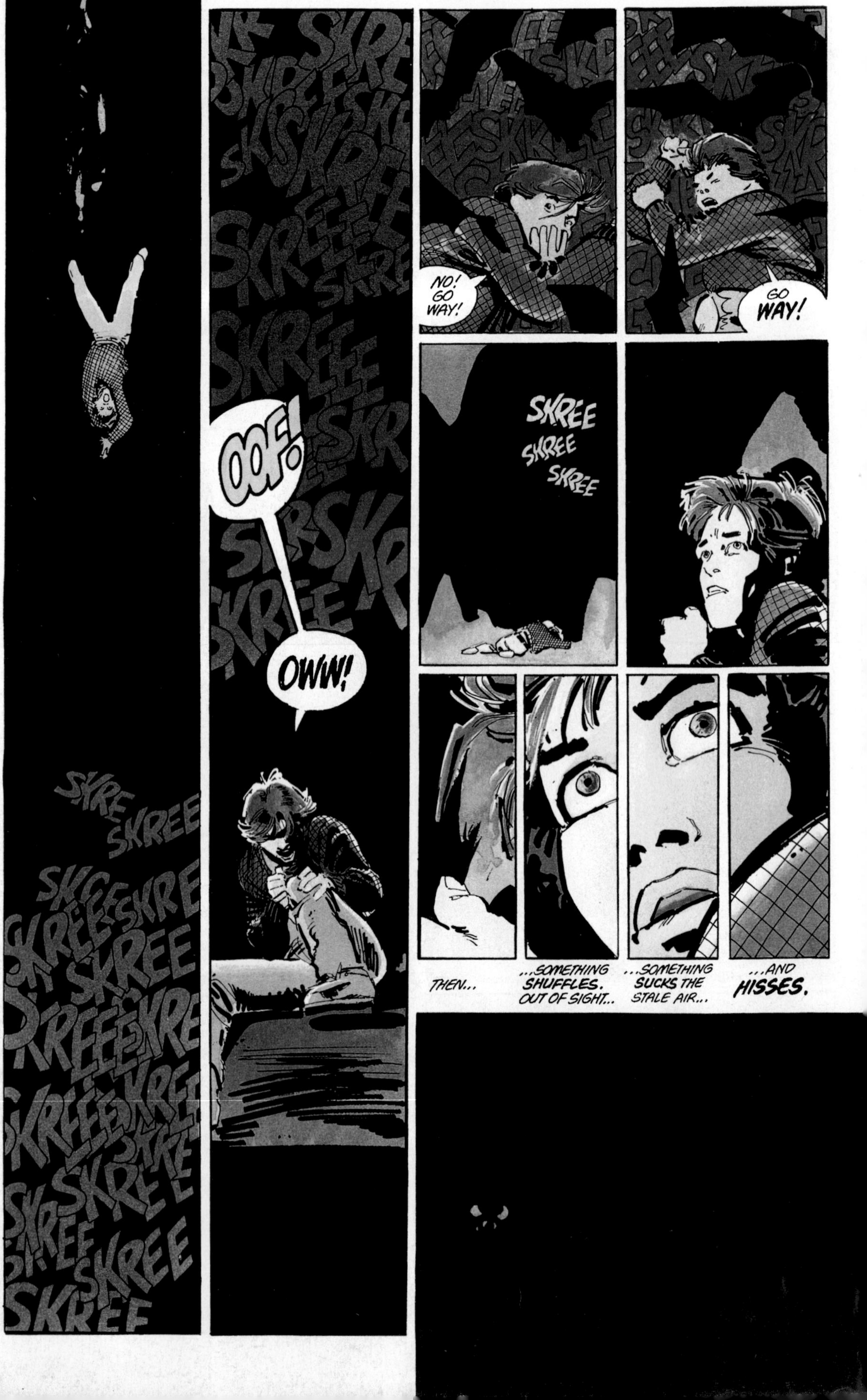
SKREE
SKREE
OOF!
OWW!
NO! GO WAY!
GO WAY!
SKREE
SKREE
SKREE
THEN...
...SOMETHING SHUFFLES. OUT OF SIGHT...
...SOMETHING SUCKS THE STALE AIR...
...AND HISSES.

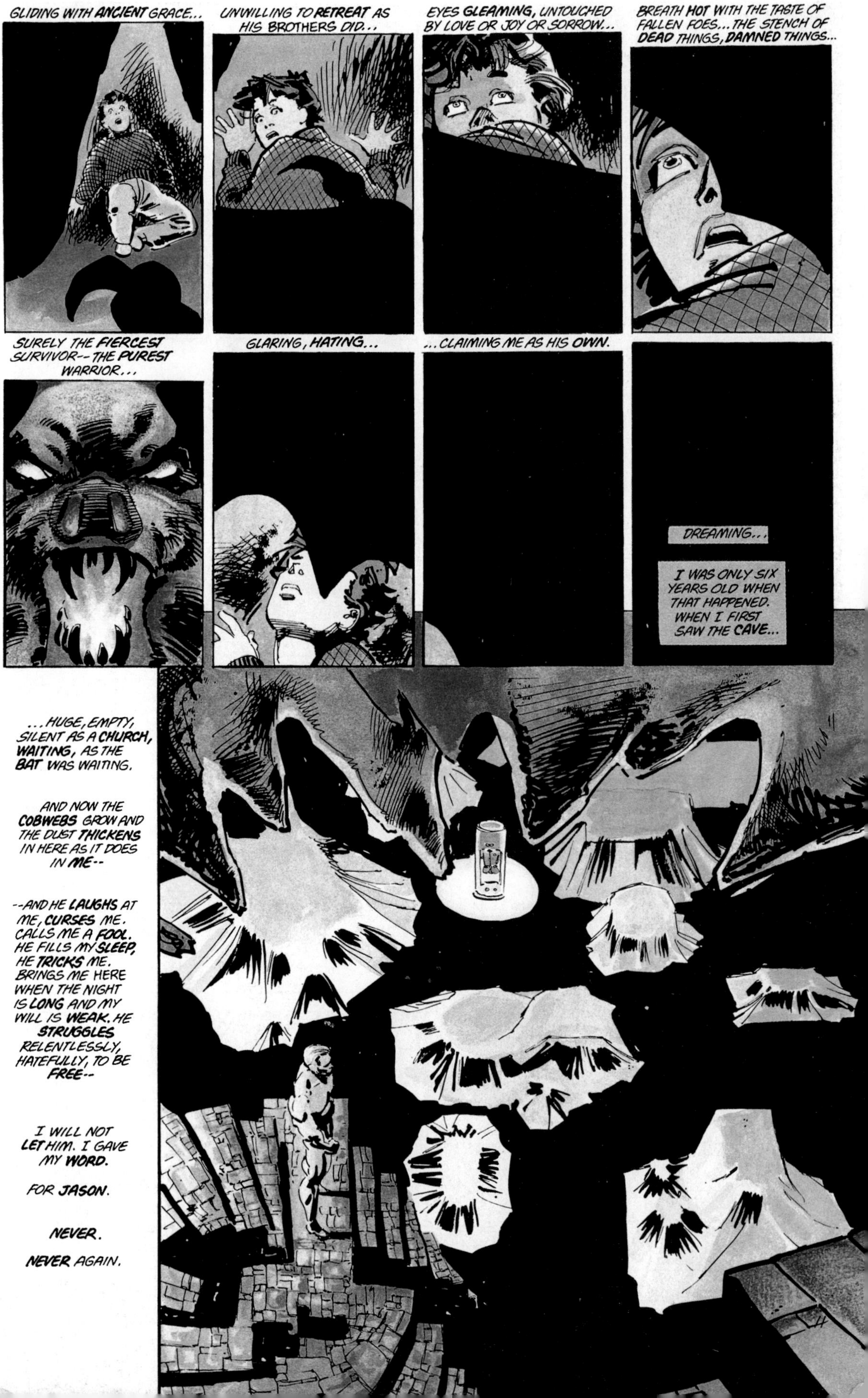
GLIDING WITH ANCIENT GRACE...
UNWILLING TO RETREAT AS HIS BROTHERS DID...
EYES GLEAMING, UNTOUCHED BY LOVE OR JOY OR SORROW...
BREATH HOT WITH THE TASTE OF FALLEN FOES... THE STENCH OF DEAD THINGS, DAMNED THINGS...
SURELY THE FIERCEST SURVIVOR-- THE PUREST WARRIOR...
GLARING, HATING...
...CLAIMING ME AS HIS OWN.
DREAMING...
I WAS ONLY SIX YEARS OLD WHEN THAT HAPPENED. WHEN I FIRST SAW THE CAVE...
...HUGE, EMPTY, SILENT AS A CHURCH, WAITING, AS THE BAT WAS WAITING.
AND NOW THE COBWEBS GROW AND THE DUST THICKENS IN HERE AS IT DOES IN ME--
--AND HE LAUGHS AT ME, CURSES ME. CALLS ME A FOOL. HE FILLS MY SLEEP, HE TRICKS ME. BRINGS ME HERE WHEN THE NIGHT IS LONG AND MY WILL IS WEAK. HE STRUGGLES RELENTLESSLY, HATEFULLY, TO BE FREE--
I WILL NOT LET HIM. I GAVE MY WORD.
FOR JASON.
NEVER.
NEVER AGAIN.

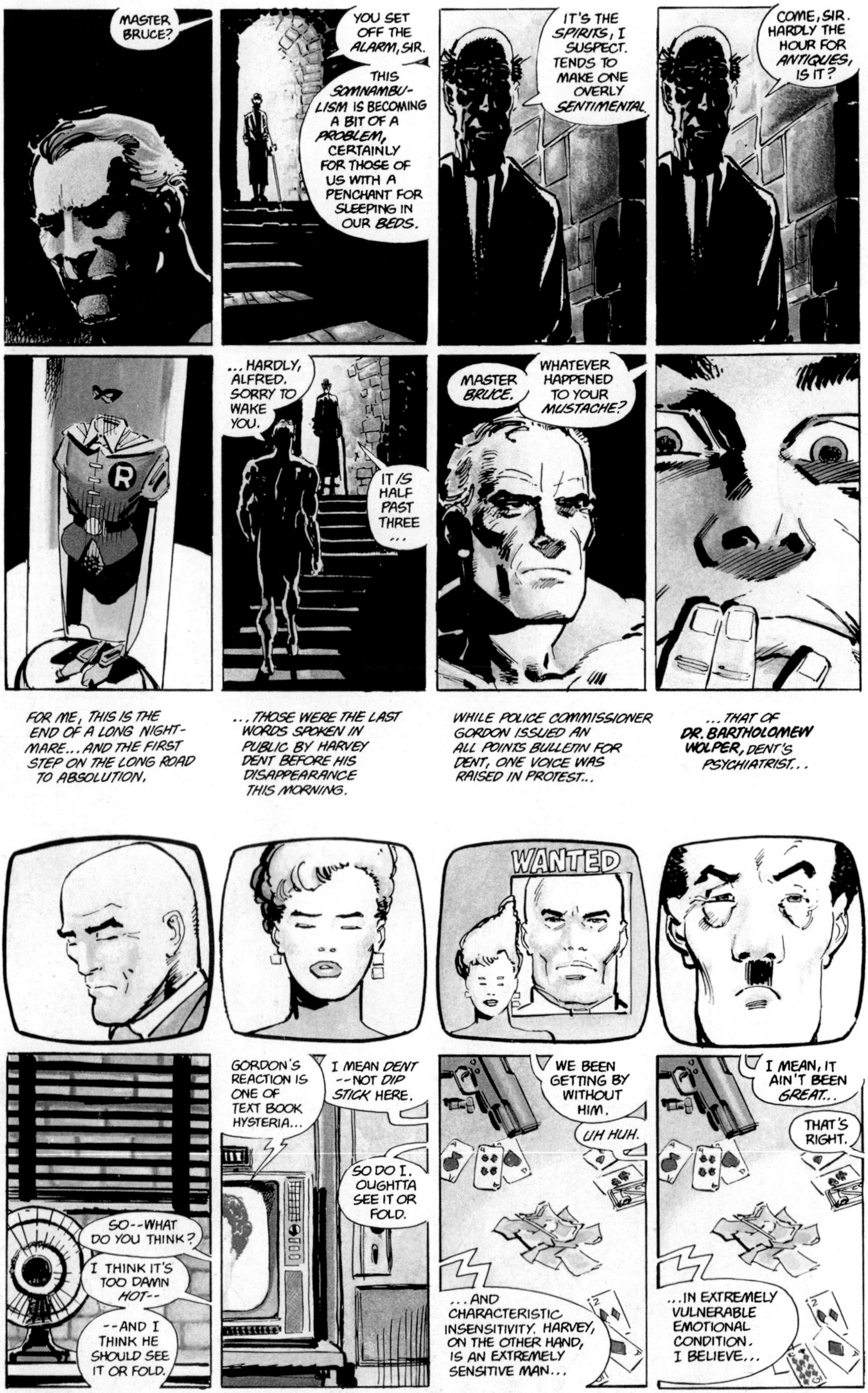
MASTER BRUCE?
YOU SET OFF THE ALARM, SIR.
THIS SOMNAMBULISM IS BECOMING A BIT OF A PROBLEM, CERTAINLY FOR THOSE OF US WITH A PENCHANT FOR SLEEPING IN OUR BEDS.
IT'S THE SPIRITS, I SUSPECT. TENDS TO MAKE ONE OVERLY SENTIMENTAL.
COME, SIR. HARDLY THE HOUR FOR ANTIQUES, IS IT?
R
...HARDLY, ALFRED. SORRY TO WAKE YOU.
IT IS HALF PAST THREE ...
MASTER BRUCE.
WHATEVER HAPPENED TO YOUR MUSTACHE?
FOR ME, THIS IS THE END OF A LONG NIGHTMARE... AND THE FIRST STEP ON THE LONG ROAD TO ABSOLUTION.
...THOSE WERE THE LAST WORDS SPOKEN IN PUBLIC BY HARVEY DENT BEFORE HIS DISAPPEARANCE THIS MORNING.
WHILE POLICE COMMISSIONER GORDON ISSUED AN ALL POINTS BULLETIN FOR DENT, ONE VOICE WAS RAISED IN PROTEST...
...THAT OF DR. BARTHOLOMEW WOLPER, DENT'S PSYCHIATRIST...
WANTED
SO--WHAT DO YOU THINK?
I THINK IT'S TOO DAMN HOT--
--AND I THINK HE SHOULD SEE IT OR FOLD.
GORDON'S REACTION IS ONE OF TEXT BOOK HYSTERIA...
I MEAN DENT --NOT DIP STICK HERE.
SO DO I. OUGHTTA SEE IT OR FOLD.
WE BEEN GETTING BY WITHOUT HIM.
UH HUH.
...AND CHARACTERISTIC INSENSITIVITY. HARVEY, ON THE OTHER HAND, IS AN EXTREMELY SENSITIVE MAN...
I MEAN, IT AIN'T BEEN GREAT...
THAT'S RIGHT.
...IN EXTREMELY VULNERABLE EMOTIONAL CONDITION. I BELIEVE...

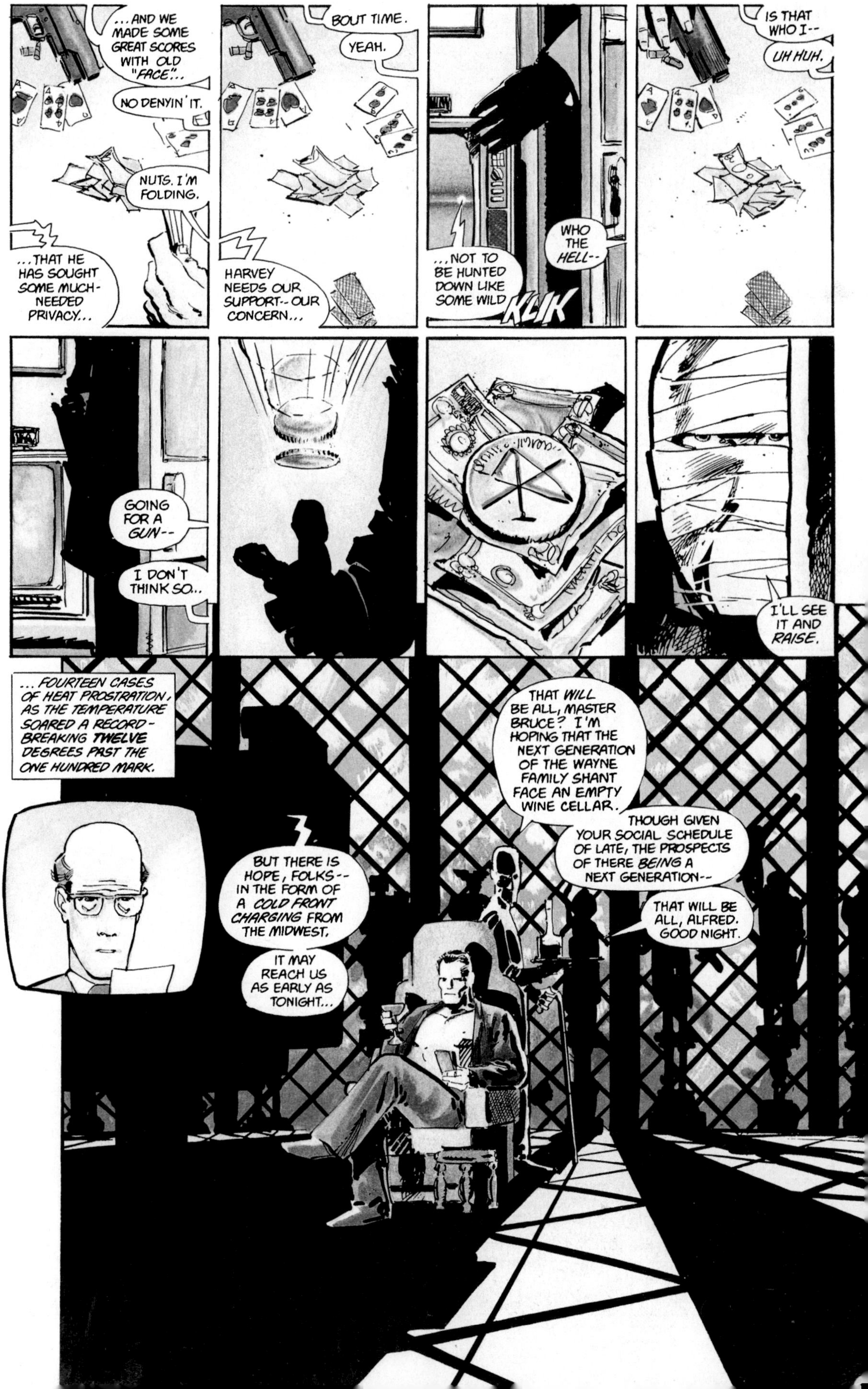
...AND WE MADE SOME GREAT SCORES WITH OLD "FACE"...
NO DENYIN' IT.
NUTS. I'M FOLDING.
...THAT HE HAS SOUGHT SOME MUCH-NEEDED PRIVACY...
BOUT TIME.
YEAH.
HARVEY NEEDS OUR SUPPORT--OUR CONCERN...
...NOT TO BE HUNTED DOWN LIKE SOME WILD
KLIK
WHO THE HELL--
IS THAT WHO I--
UH HUH.
GOING FOR A GUN--
I DON'T THINK SO...
I'LL SEE IT AND RAISE.
...FOURTEEN CASES OF HEAT PROSTRATION, AS THE TEMPERATURE SOARED A RECORD-BREAKING TWELVE DEGREES PAST THE ONE HUNDRED MARK.
BUT THERE IS HOPE, FOLKS--IN THE FORM OF A COLD FRONT CHARGING FROM THE MIDWEST.
IT MAY REACH US AS EARLY AS TONIGHT...
THAT WILL BE ALL, MASTER BRUCE? I'M HOPING THAT THE NEXT GENERATION OF THE WAYNE FAMILY SHANT FACE AN EMPTY WINE CELLAR.
THOUGH GIVEN YOUR SOCIAL SCHEDULE OF LATE, THE PROSPECTS OF THERE BEING A NEXT GENERATION--
THAT WILL BE ALL, ALFRED. GOOD NIGHT.

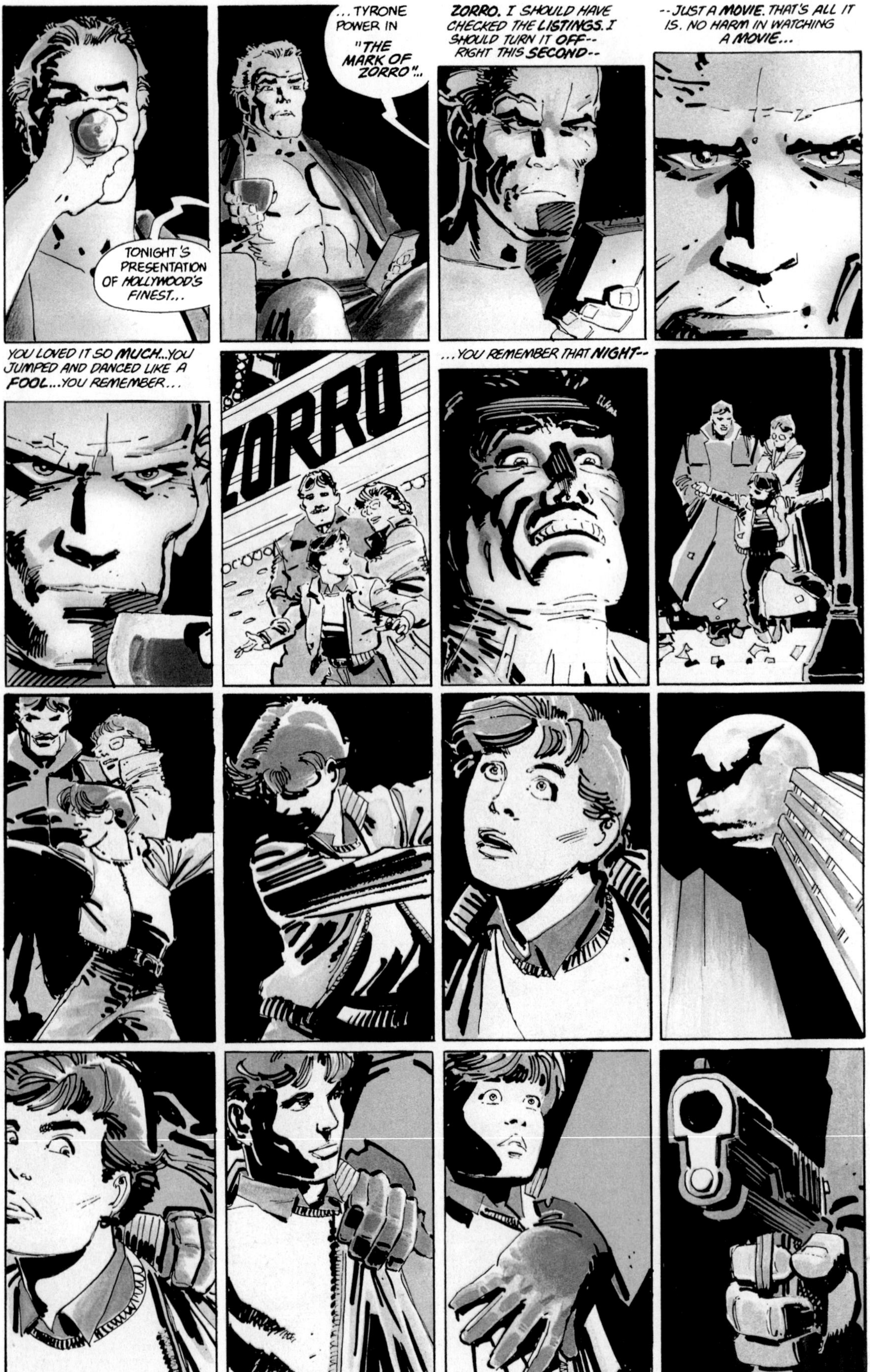
TONIGHT'S PRESENTATION OF HOLLYWOOD'S FINEST...
...TYRONE POWER IN "THE MARK OF ZORRO"...
ZORRO. I SHOULD HAVE CHECKED THE LISTINGS. I SHOULD TURN IT OFF-- RIGHT THIS SECOND--
--JUST A MOVIE. THAT'S ALL IT IS. NO HARM IN WATCHING A MOVIE...
YOU LOVED IT SO MUCH...YOU JUMPED AND DANCED LIKE A FOOL...YOU REMEMBER...
ZORRO
...YOU REMEMBER THAT NIGHT--

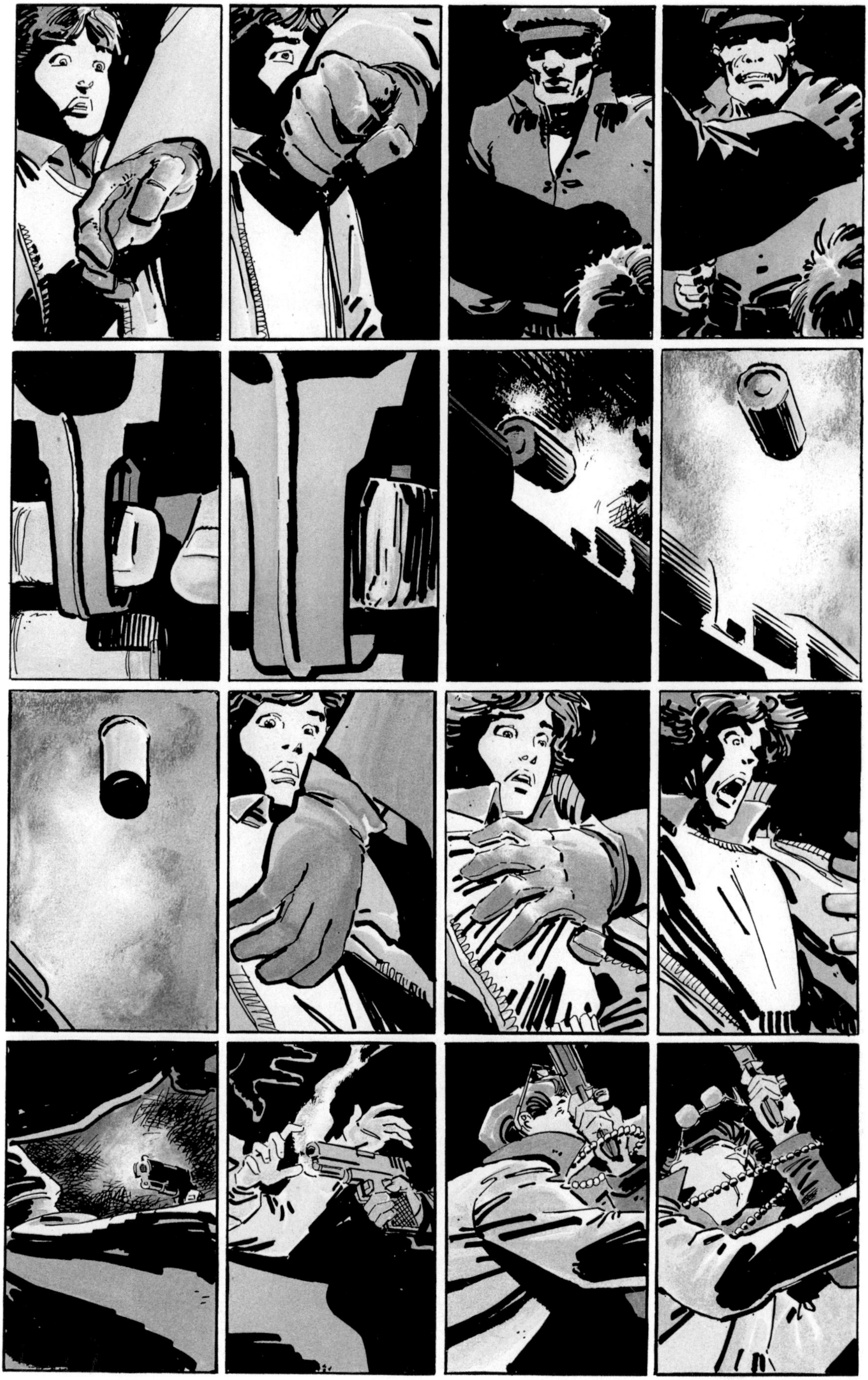

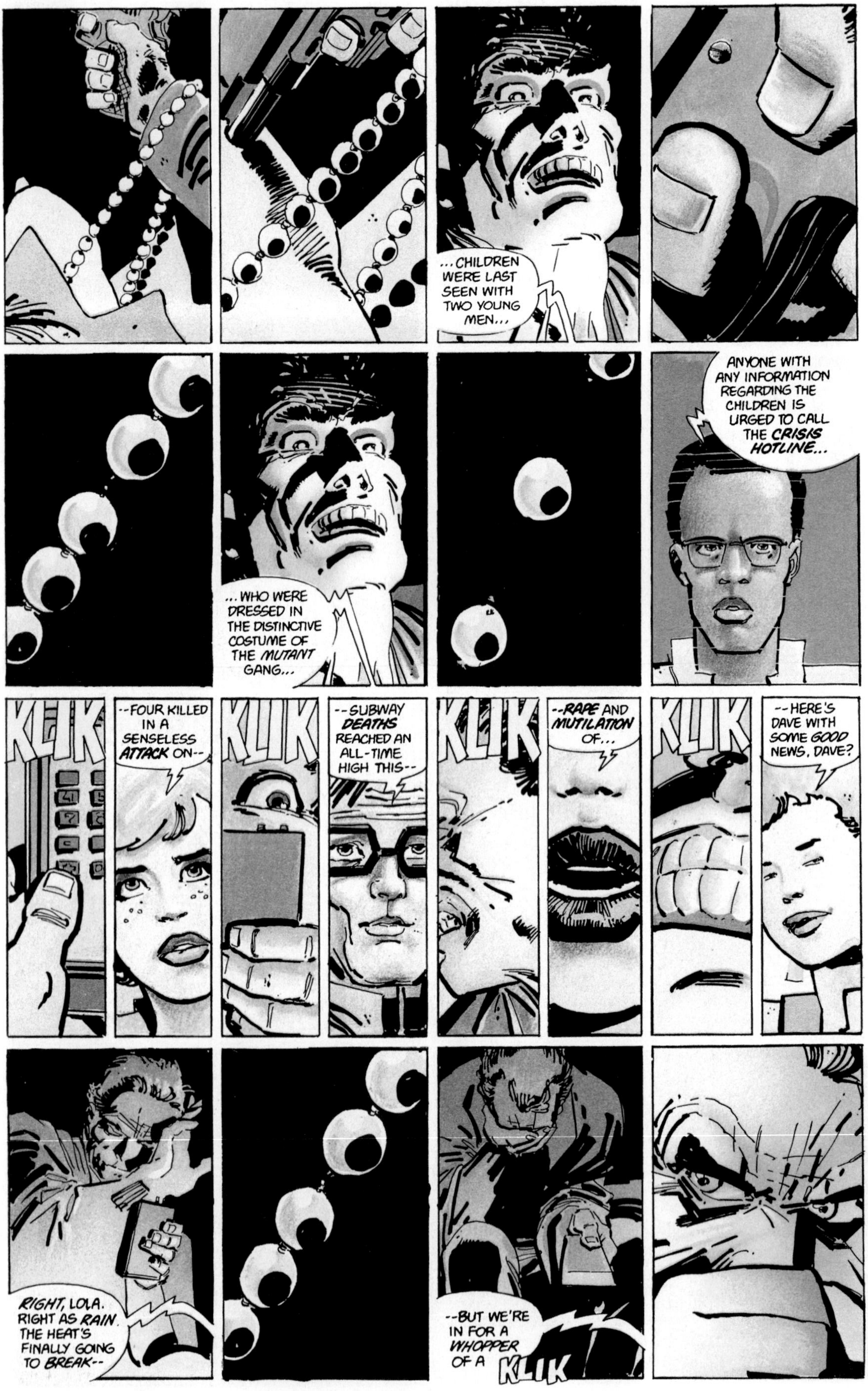
...CHILDREN WERE LAST SEEN WITH TWO YOUNG MEN...
...WHO WERE DRESSED IN THE DISTINCTIVE COSTUME OF THE MUTANT GANG...
ANYONE WITH ANY INFORMATION REGARDING THE CHILDREN IS URGED TO CALL THE CRISIS HOTLINE...
KLIK
--FOUR KILLED IN A SENSELESS ATTACK ON--
KLIK
--SUBWAY DEATHS REACHED AN ALL-TIME HIGH THIS--
KLIK
--RAPE AND MUTILATION OF...
KLIK
--HERE'S DAVE WITH SOME GOOD NEWS, DAVE?
RIGHT, LOLA. RIGHT AS RAIN. THE HEAT'S FINALLY GOING TO BREAK--
--BUT WE'RE IN FOR A WHOPPER OF A
KLIK

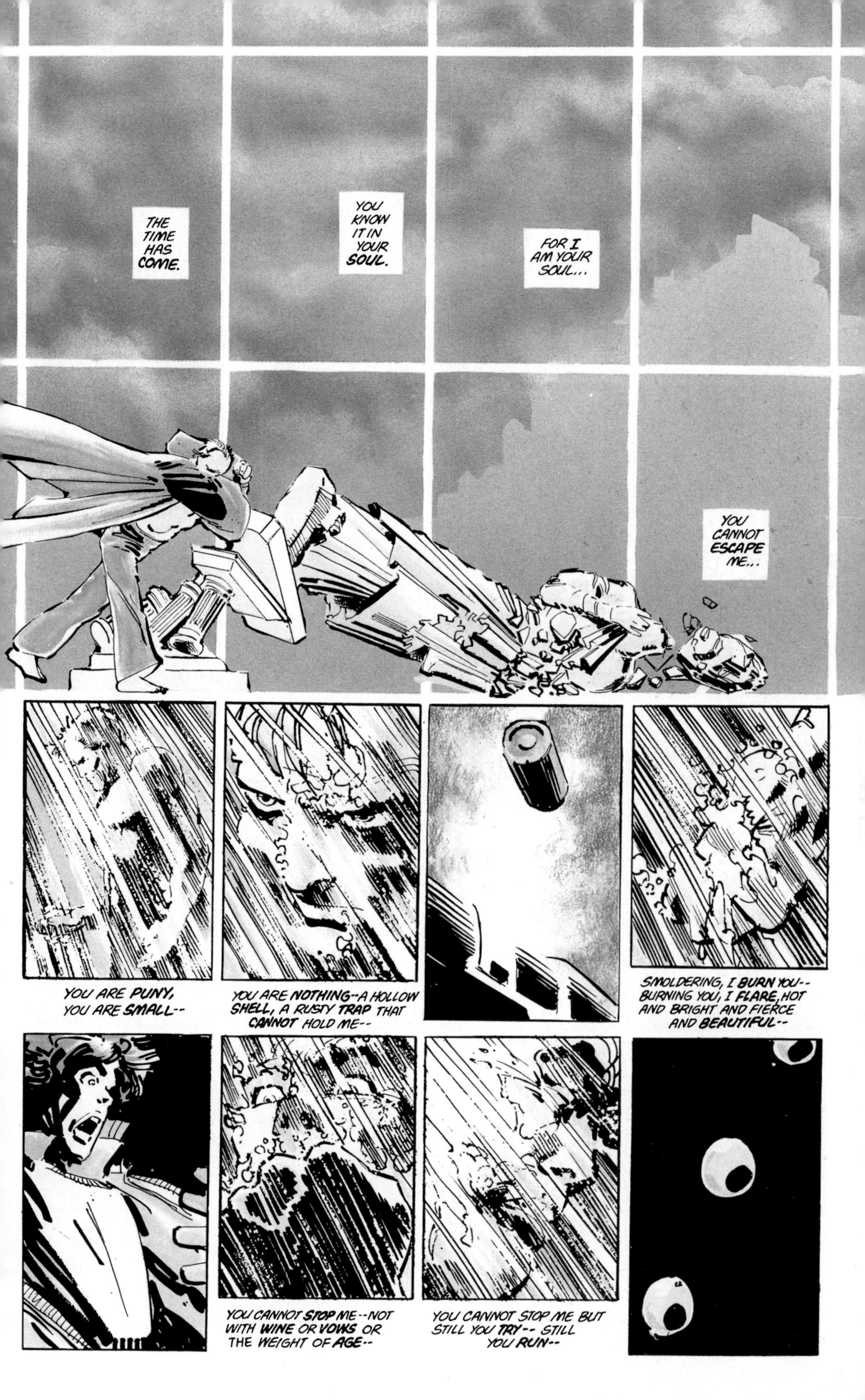
THE TIME HAS COME.
YOU KNOW IT IN YOUR SOUL.
FOR I AM YOUR SOUL...
YOU CANNOT ESCAPE ME...
YOU ARE PUNY, YOU ARE SMALL--
YOU ARE NOTHING--A HOLLOW SHELL, A RUSTY TRAP THAT CANNOT HOLD ME--
SMOLDERING, I BURN YOU--BURNING YOU, I FLARE, HOT AND BRIGHT AND FIERCE AND BEAUTIFUL--
YOU CANNOT STOP ME--NOT WITH WINE OR VOWS OR THE WEIGHT OF AGE--
YOU CANNOT STOP ME BUT STILL YOU TRY-- STILL YOU RUN--

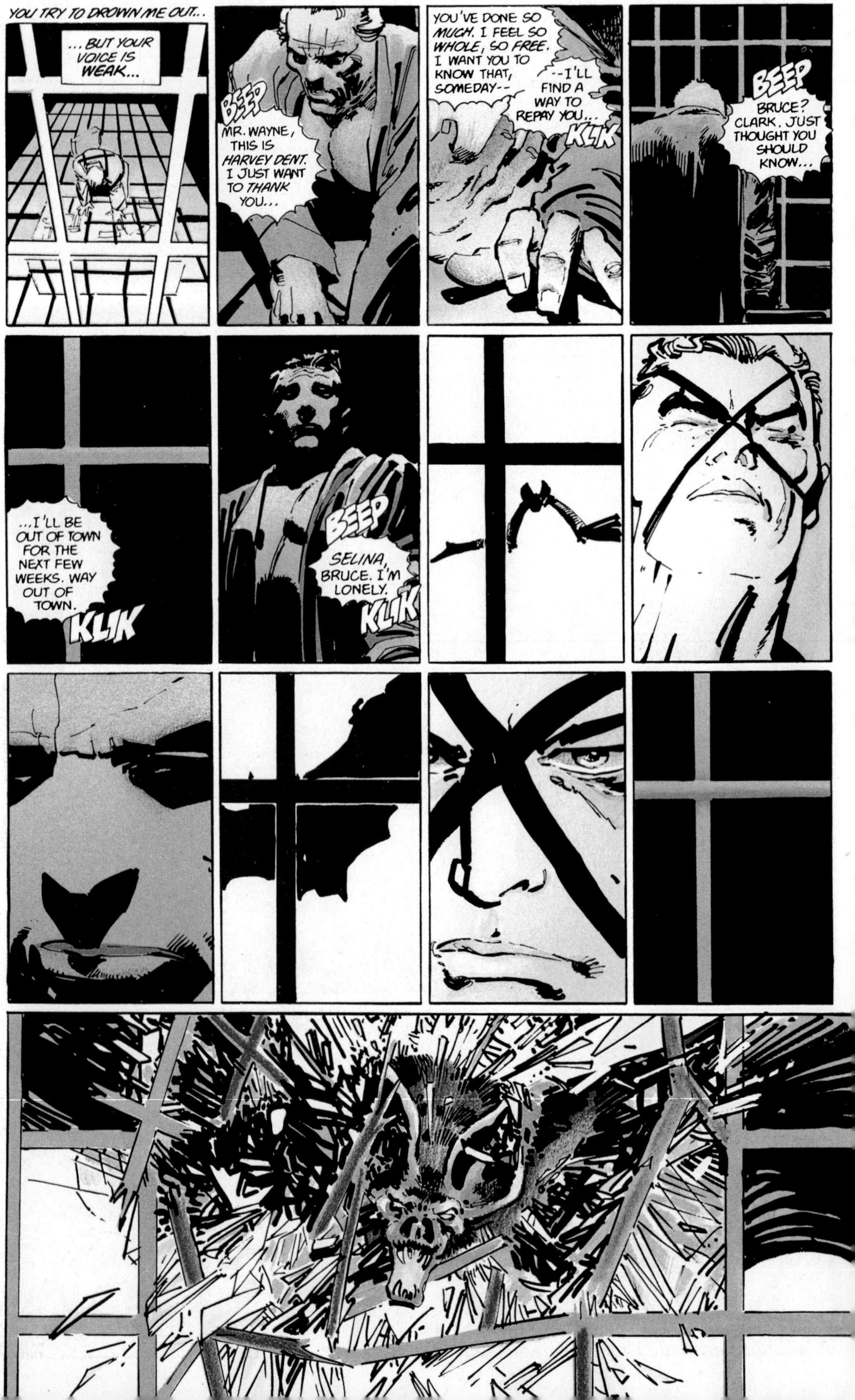
YOU TRY TO DROWN ME OUT...
...BUT YOUR VOICE IS WEAK...
BEEP
MR. WAYNE, THIS IS HARVEY DENT. I JUST WANT TO THANK YOU...
YOU'VE DONE SO MUCH. I FEEL SO WHOLE, SO FREE. I WANT YOU TO KNOW THAT, SOMEDAY--
--I'LL FIND A WAY TO REPAY YOU...
KLIK
BEEP
BRUCE? CLARK. JUST THOUGHT YOU SHOULD KNOW...
...I'LL BE OUT OF TOWN FOR THE NEXT FEW WEEKS. WAY OUT OF TOWN.
KLIK
BEEP
SELINA, BRUCE. I'M LONELY.
KLIK

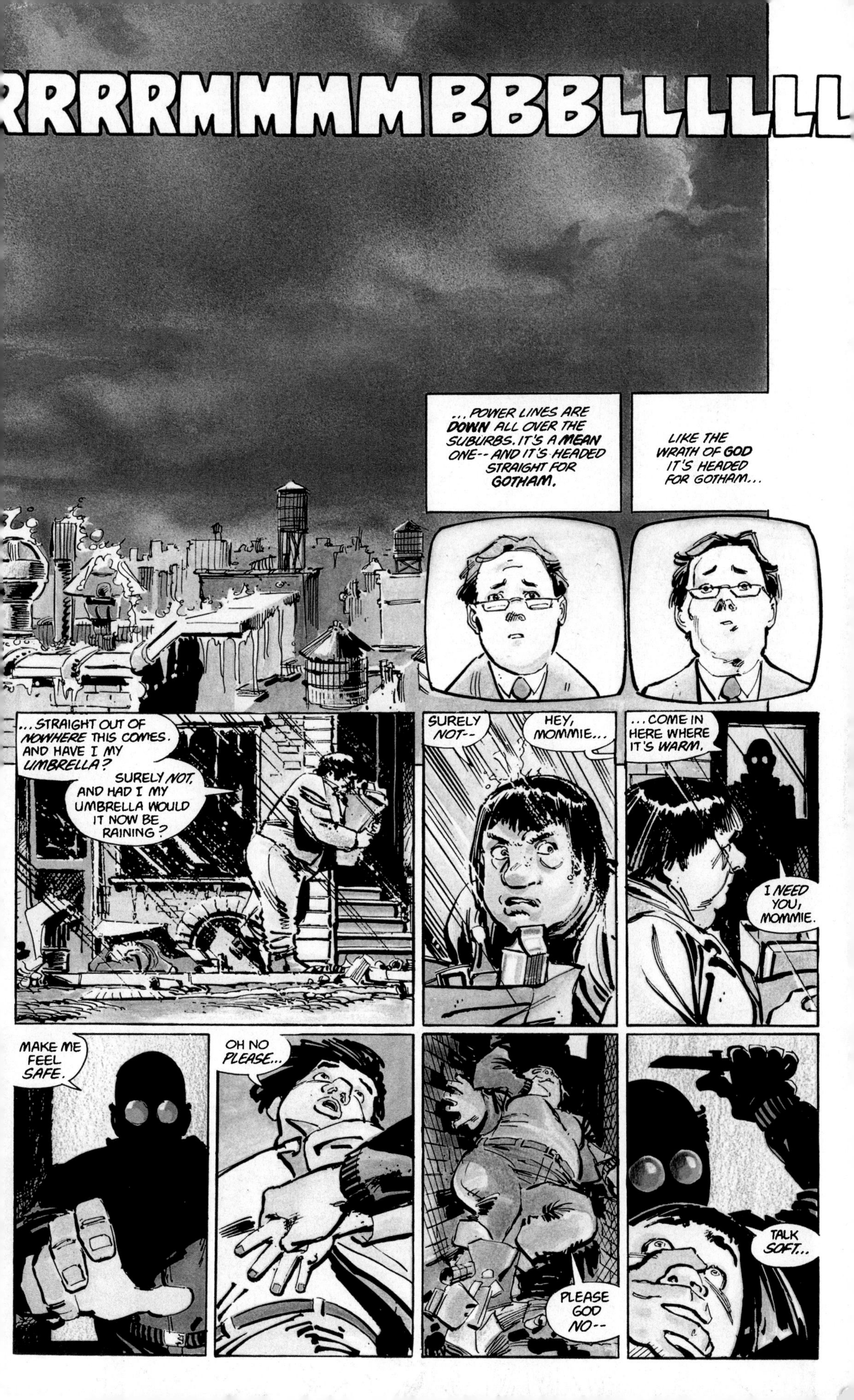
RRRRMMMMMBBBLLLLL
...POWER LINES ARE DOWN ALL OVER THE SUBURBS. IT'S A MEAN ONE-- AND IT'S HEADED STRAIGHT FOR GOTHAM.
LIKE THE WRATH OF GOD IT'S HEADED FOR GOTHAM...
...STRAIGHT OUT OF NOWHERE THIS COMES. AND HAVE I MY UMBRELLA?
SURELY NOT. AND HAD I MY UMBRELLA WOULD IT NOW BE RAINING?
SURELY NOT--
HEY, MOMMIE...
...COME IN HERE WHERE IT'S WARM.
I NEED YOU, MOMMIE.
MAKE ME FEEL SAFE.
OH NO PLEASE...
PLEASE GOD NO--
TALK SOFT...

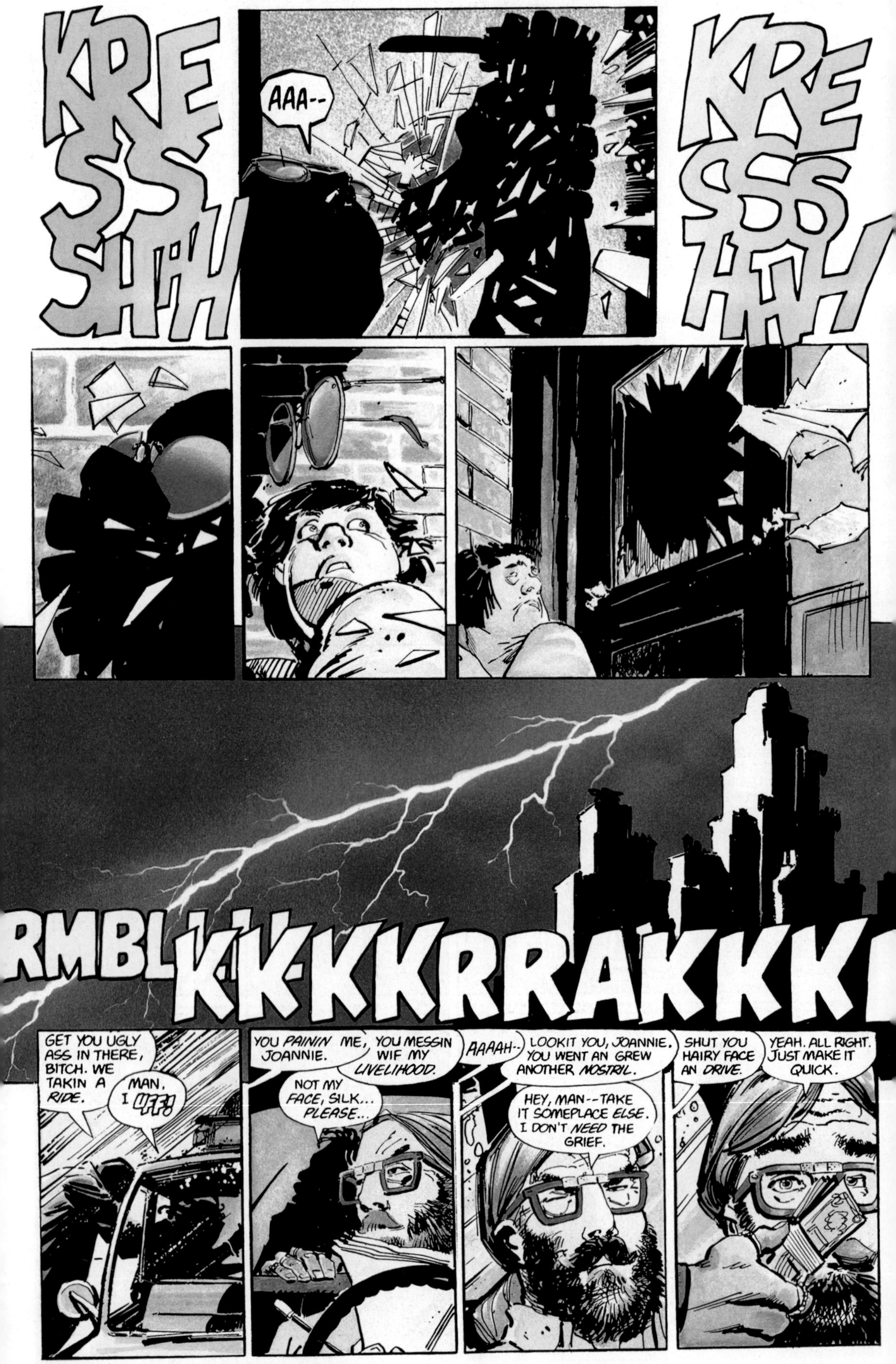
KRESSSHHH
AAA--
KRESSSHHH
RMBL
KKKKRRAKKK
GET YOU UGLY ASS IN THERE, BITCH. WE TAKIN A RIDE.
MAN, I OFF!
YOU PAININ ME, JOANNIE.
YOU MESSIN WIF MY LIVELIHOOD.
NOT MY FACE, SILK... PLEASE...
AAAAH--
LOOKIT YOU, JOANNIE. YOU WENT AN GREW ANOTHER NOSTRIL.
HEY, MAN--TAKE IT SOMEPLACE ELSE. I DON'T NEED THE GRIEF.
SHUT YOU HAIRY FACE AN DRIVE.
YEAH. ALL RIGHT. JUST MAKE IT QUICK.

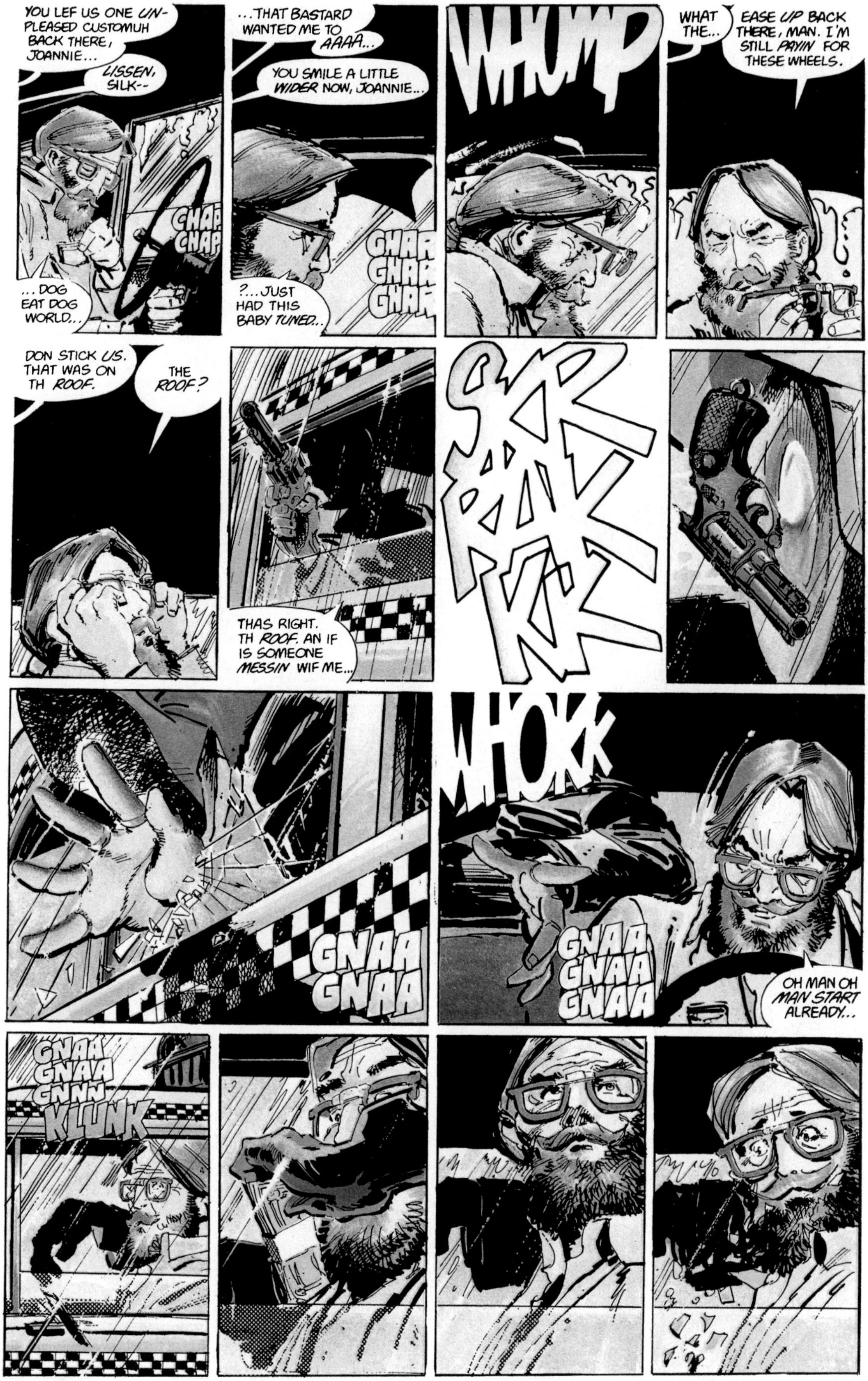

YOU LEF US ONE UN-PLEASED CUSTOMUH BACK THERE, JOANNIE...
LISSEN, SILK--
CHAP CHAP
... DOG EAT DOG WORLD...
...THAT BASTARD WANTED ME TO AAAA...
YOU SMILE A LITTLE WIDER NOW, JOANNIE...
GHAR GHAR GHAR
?...JUST HAD THIS BABY TUNED...
WHUMP
WHAT THE...
EASE UP BACK THERE, MAN. I'M STILL PAYIN FOR THESE WHEELS.
DON STICK US. THAT WAS ON TH ROOF.
THE ROOF?
THAS RIGHT. TH ROOF. AN IF IS SOMEONE MESSIN WIF ME...
SKRRAKK
GNAA GNAA
WHOKK
GNAA GNAA GNAA
OH MAN OH MAN START ALREADY...
GNAA GNAA GNNN
KLUNK

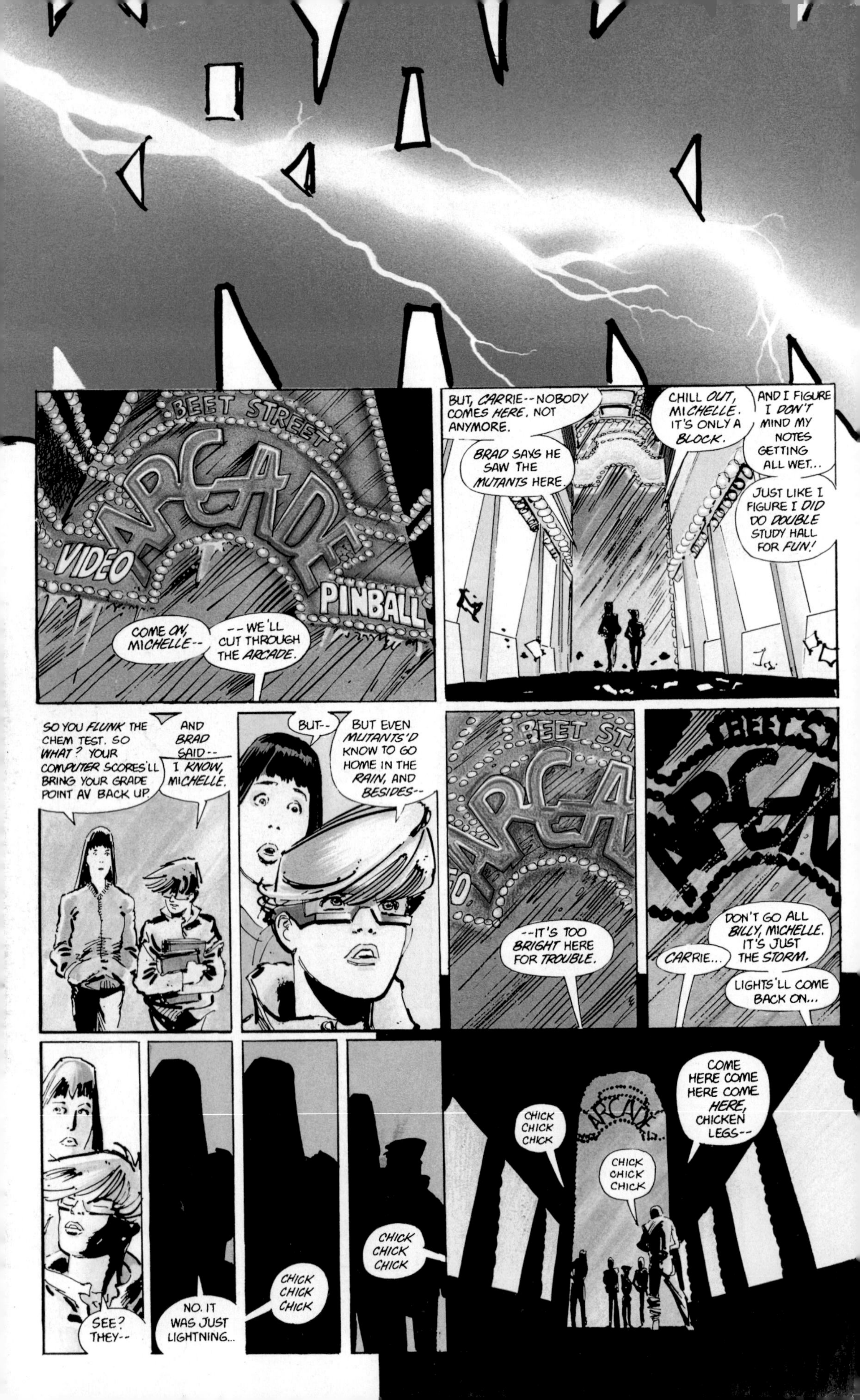
BEET STREET
VIDEO ARCADE PINBALL
COME ON, MICHELLE--
--WE'LL CUT THROUGH THE ARCADE.
BUT, CARRIE--NOBODY COMES HERE. NOT ANYMORE.
BRAD SAYS HE SAW THE MUTANTS HERE.
CHILL OUT, MICHELLE. IT'S ONLY A BLOCK.
AND I FIGURE I DON'T MIND MY NOTES GETTING ALL WET...
JUST LIKE I FIGURE I DID DO DOUBLE STUDY HALL FOR FUN!
SO YOU FLUNK THE CHEM TEST. SO WHAT? YOUR COMPUTER SCORES'LL BRING YOUR GRADE POINT AV BACK UP.
AND BRAD SAID--
I KNOW, MICHELLE.
BUT--
BUT EVEN MUTANTS'D KNOW TO GO HOME IN THE RAIN, AND BESIDES--
--IT'S TOO BRIGHT HERE FOR TROUBLE.
CARRIE...
DON'T GO ALL BILLY, MICHELLE. IT'S JUST THE STORM.
LIGHTS'LL COME BACK ON...
SEE? THEY--
NO. IT WAS JUST LIGHTNING...
CHICK CHICK CHICK
CHICK CHICK CHICK
CHICK CHICK CHICK
CHICK CHICK CHICK
COME HERE COME HERE COME HERE, CHICKEN LEGS--

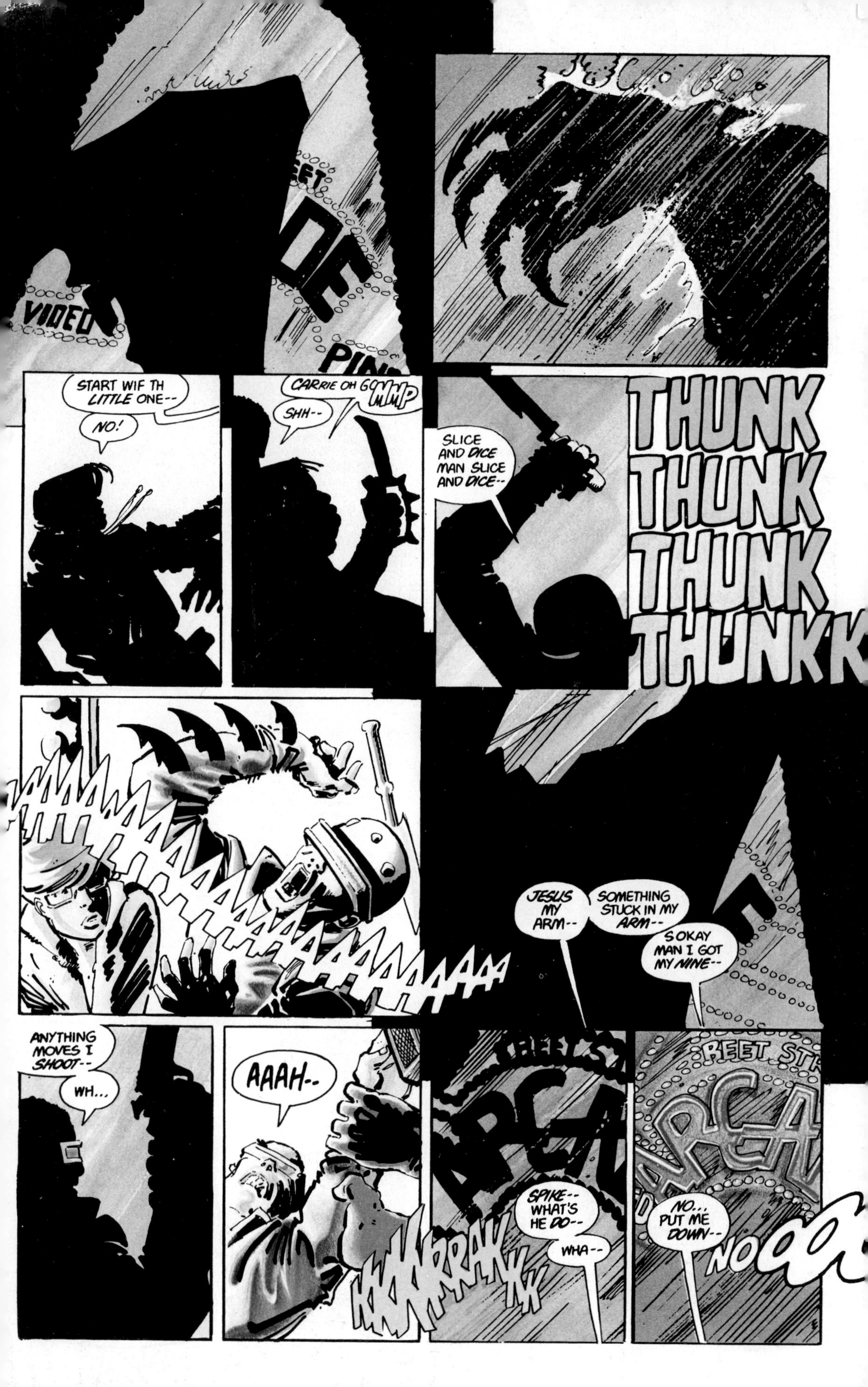

START WIF TH LITTLE ONE--
NO!
CARRIE OH GO MMP
SHH--
SLICE AND DICE MAN SLICE AND DICE--
THUNK
THUNK
THUNK
THUNKK
JESUS MY ARM--
SOMETHING STUCK IN MY ARM--
S OKAY MAN I GOT MY NINE--
ANYTHING MOVES I SHOOT--
WH...
AAAH--
KRAAKRAKKK
SPIKE-- WHAT'S HE DO--
WHA--
NO... PUT ME DOWN--
NOOO

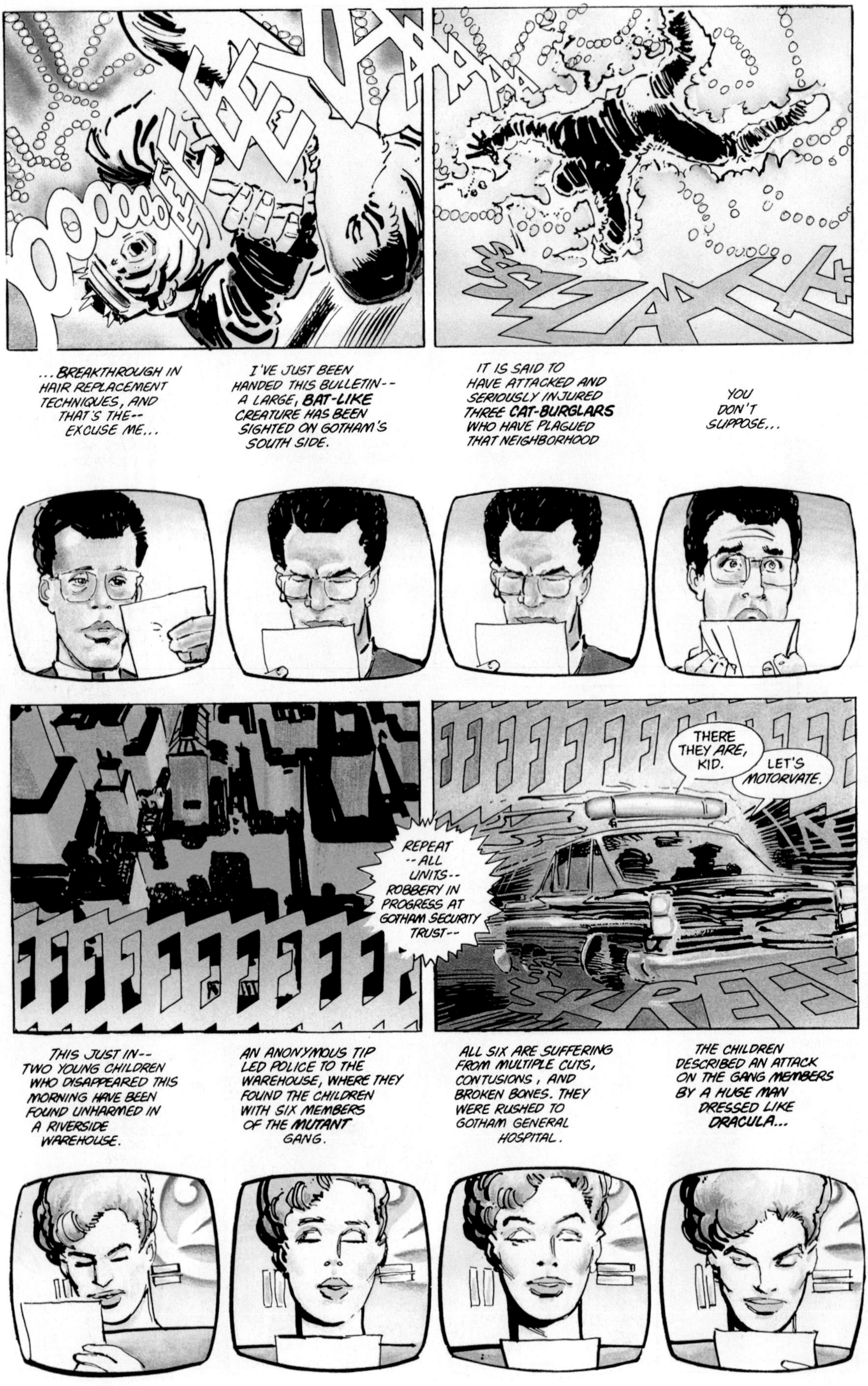
...BREAKTHROUGH IN HAIR REPLACEMENT TECHNIQUES, AND THAT'S THE-- EXCUSE ME...
I'VE JUST BEEN HANDED THIS BULLETIN-- A LARGE, BAT-LIKE CREATURE HAS BEEN SIGHTED ON GOTHAM'S SOUTH SIDE.
IT IS SAID TO HAVE ATTACKED AND SERIOUSLY INJURED THREE CAT-BURGLARS WHO HAVE PLAGUED THAT NEIGHBORHOOD
YOU DON'T SUPPOSE...
REPEAT --ALL UNITS-- ROBBERY IN PROGRESS AT GOTHAM SECURITY TRUST--
THERE THEY ARE, KID.
LET'S MOTORVATE.
THIS JUST IN-- TWO YOUNG CHILDREN WHO DISAPPEARED THIS MORNING HAVE BEEN FOUND UNHARMED IN A RIVERSIDE WAREHOUSE.
AN ANONYMOUS TIP LED POLICE TO THE WAREHOUSE, WHERE THEY FOUND THE CHILDREN WITH SIX MEMBERS OF THE MUTANT GANG.
ALL SIX ARE SUFFERING FROM MULTIPLE CUTS, CONTUSIONS, AND BROKEN BONES. THEY WERE RUSHED TO GOTHAM GENERAL HOSPITAL.
THE CHILDREN DESCRIBED AN ATTACK ON THE GANG MEMBERS BY A HUGE MAN DRESSED LIKE DRACULA...

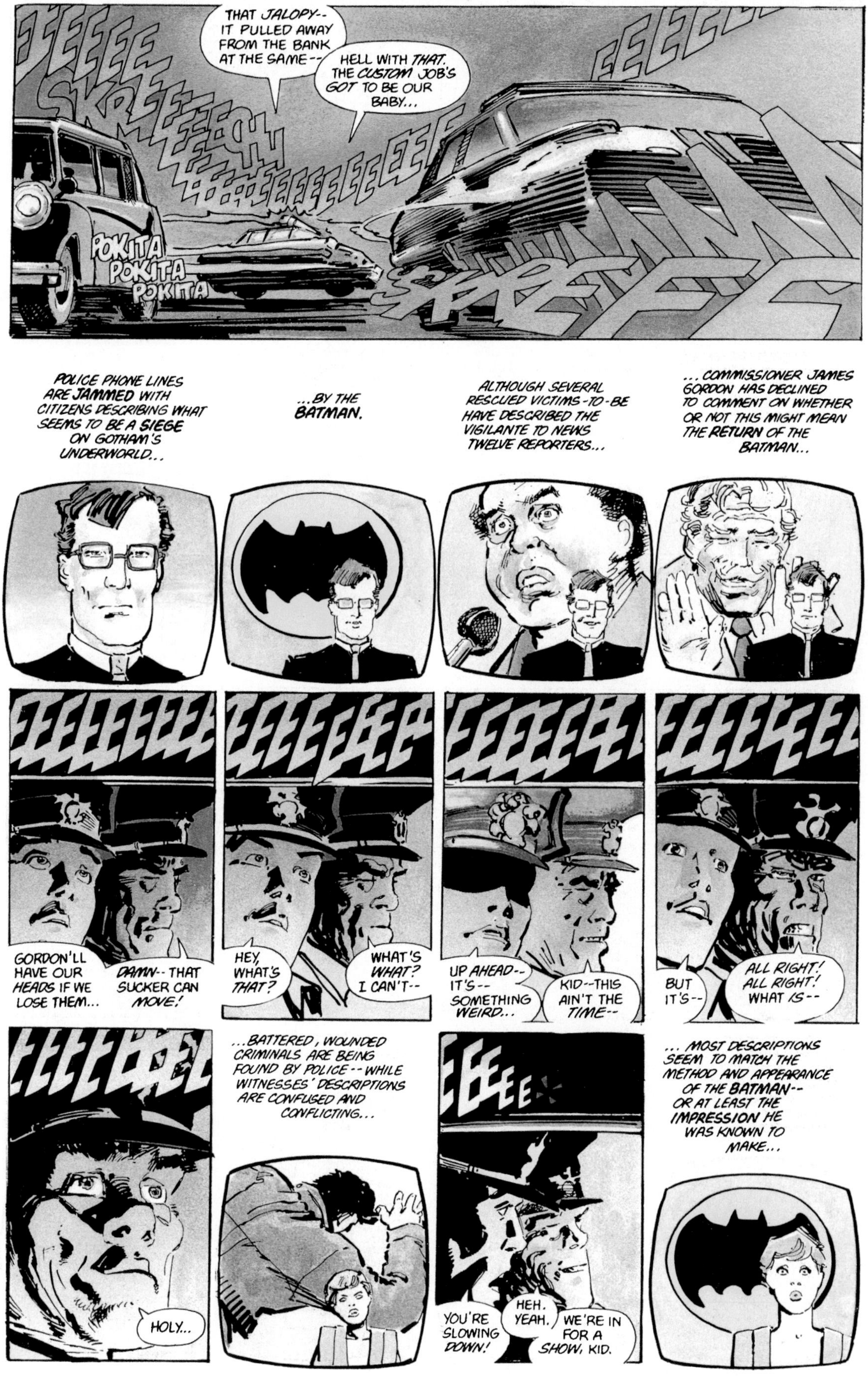
THAT JALOPY--
IT PULLED AWAY
FROM THE BANK
AT THE SAME--
HELL WITH THAT.
THE CUSTOM JOB'S
GOT TO BE OUR
BABY...
POKITA
POKITA
POKITA
POLICE PHONE LINES
ARE JAMMED WITH
CITIZENS DESCRIBING WHAT
SEEMS TO BE A SIEGE
ON GOTHAM'S
UNDERWORLD...
...BY THE
BATMAN.
ALTHOUGH SEVERAL
RESCUED VICTIMS-TO-BE
HAVE DESCRIBED THE
VIGILANTE TO NEWS
TWELVE REPORTERS...
...COMMISSIONER JAMES
GORDON HAS DECLINED
TO COMMENT ON WHETHER
OR NOT THIS MIGHT MEAN
THE RETURN OF THE
BATMAN...
GORDON'LL HAVE OUR HEADS IF WE LOSE THEM...
DAMN-- THAT SUCKER CAN MOVE!
HEY, WHAT'S THAT?
WHAT'S WHAT? I CAN'T--
UP AHEAD-- IT'S-- SOMETHING WEIRD...
KID--THIS AIN'T THE TIME--
BUT IT'S--
ALL RIGHT! ALL RIGHT! WHAT IS--
HOLY...
...BATTERED, WOUNDED
CRIMINALS ARE BEING
FOUND BY POLICE--WHILE
WITNESSES' DESCRIPTIONS
ARE CONFUSED AND
CONFLICTING...
YOU'RE SLOWING DOWN!
HEH. YEAH.
WE'RE IN FOR A SHOW, KID.
...MOST DESCRIPTIONS
SEEM TO MATCH THE
METHOD AND APPEARANCE
OF THE BATMAN--
OR AT LEAST THE
IMPRESSION HE
WAS KNOWN TO
MAKE...

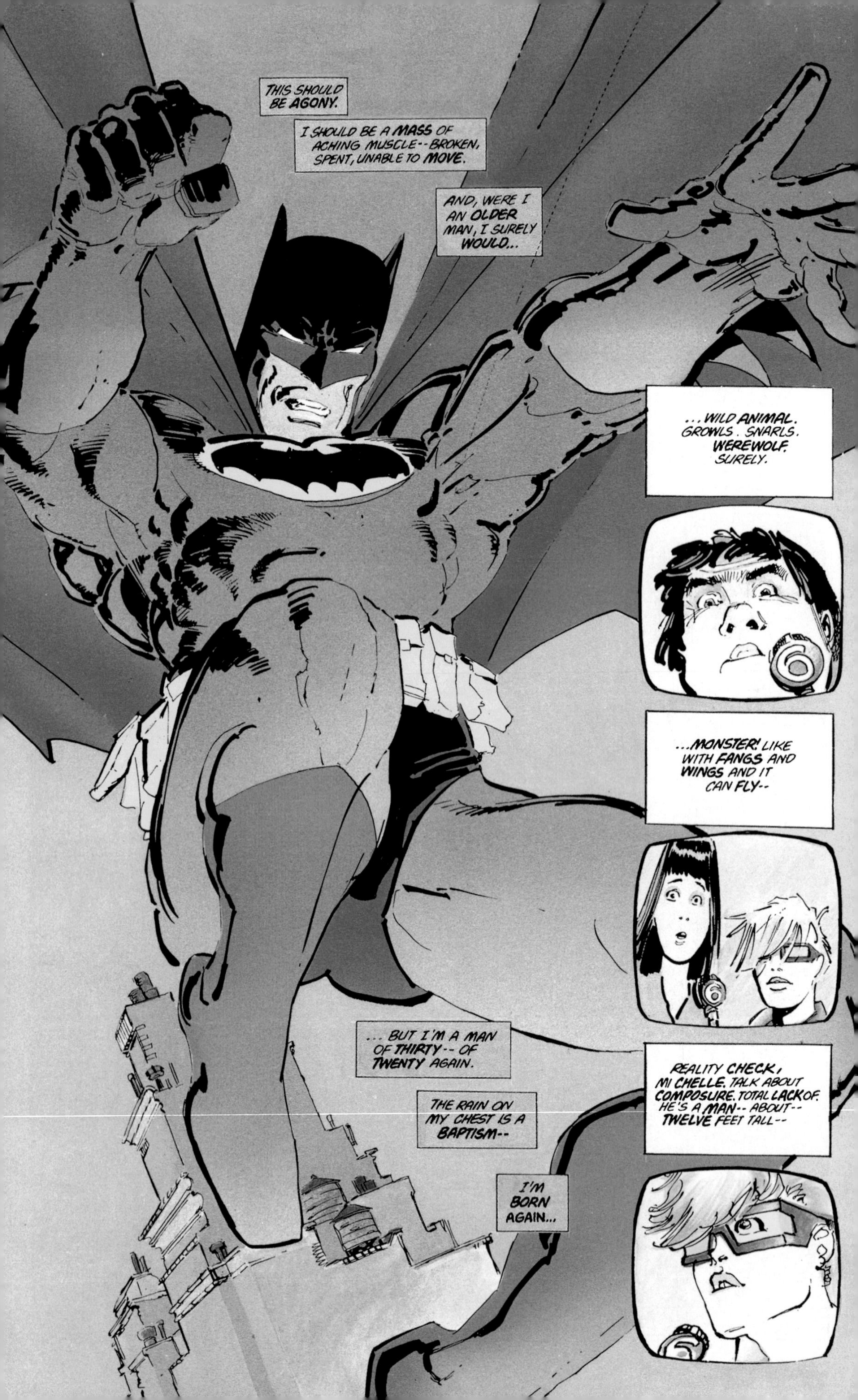
THIS SHOULD BE AGONY.
I SHOULD BE A MASS OF ACHING MUSCLE--BROKEN, SPENT, UNABLE TO MOVE.
AND, WERE I AN OLDER MAN, I SURELY WOULD...
...WILD ANIMAL. GROWLS. SNARLS. WEREWOLF. SURELY.
...MONSTER! LIKE WITH FANGS AND WINGS AND IT CAN FLY--
...BUT I'M A MAN OF THIRTY--OF TWENTY AGAIN.
THE RAIN ON MY CHEST IS A BAPTISM--
I'M BORN AGAIN...
REALITY CHECK, MI CHELLE. TALK ABOUT COMPOSURE. TOTAL LACK OF. HE'S A MAN--ABOUT--TWELVE FEET TALL--

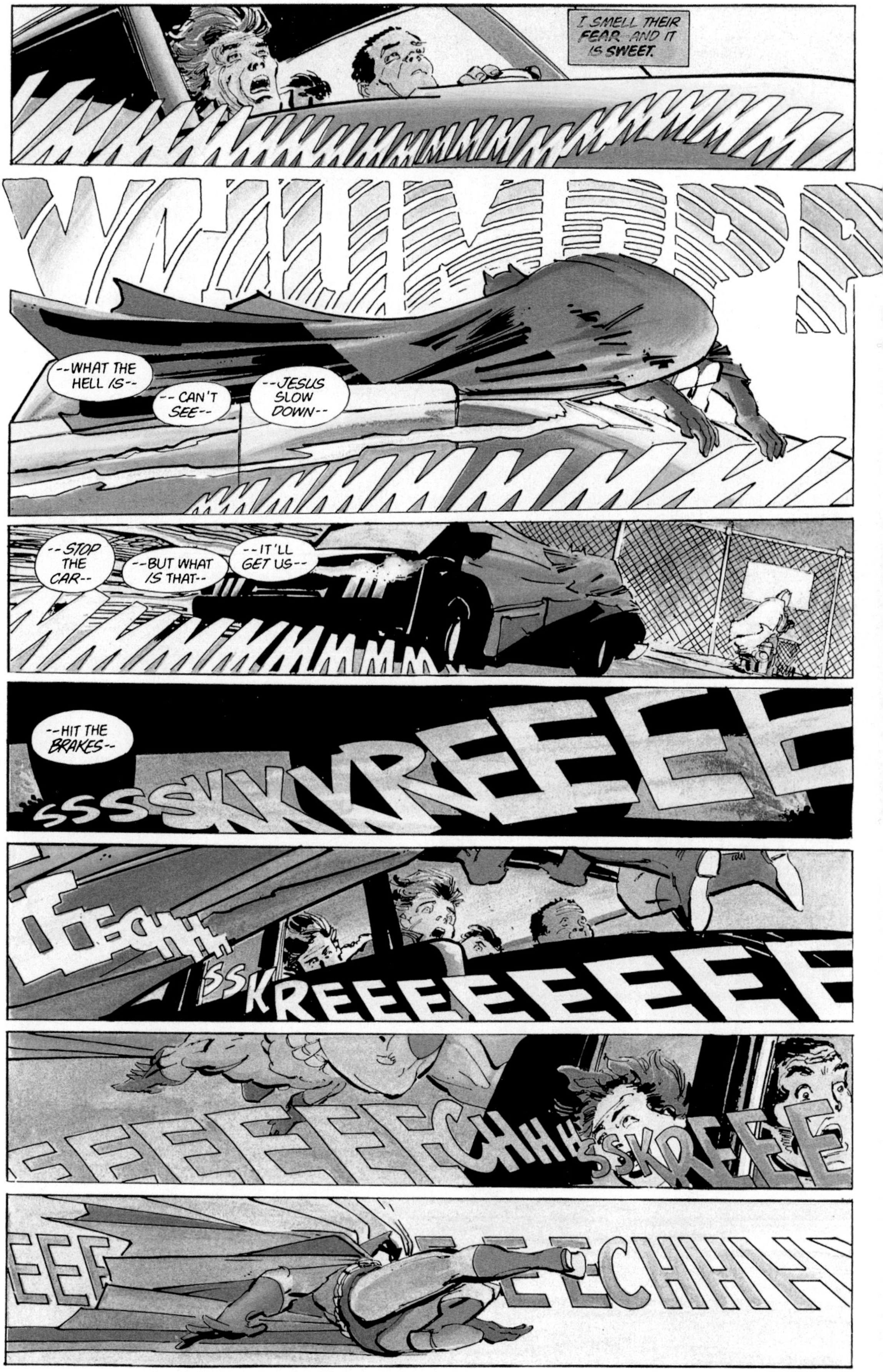

I SMELL THEIR FEAR AND IT IS SWEET.
WHUMPP
--WHAT THE HELL IS--
--CAN'T SEE--
--JESUS SLOW DOWN--
--STOP THE CAR--
--BUT WHAT IS THAT--
--IT'LL GET US--
--HIT THE BRAKES--
SSSSKKKREEEE
SSKREEEEEEEEEE
SKREEE
ECHHH

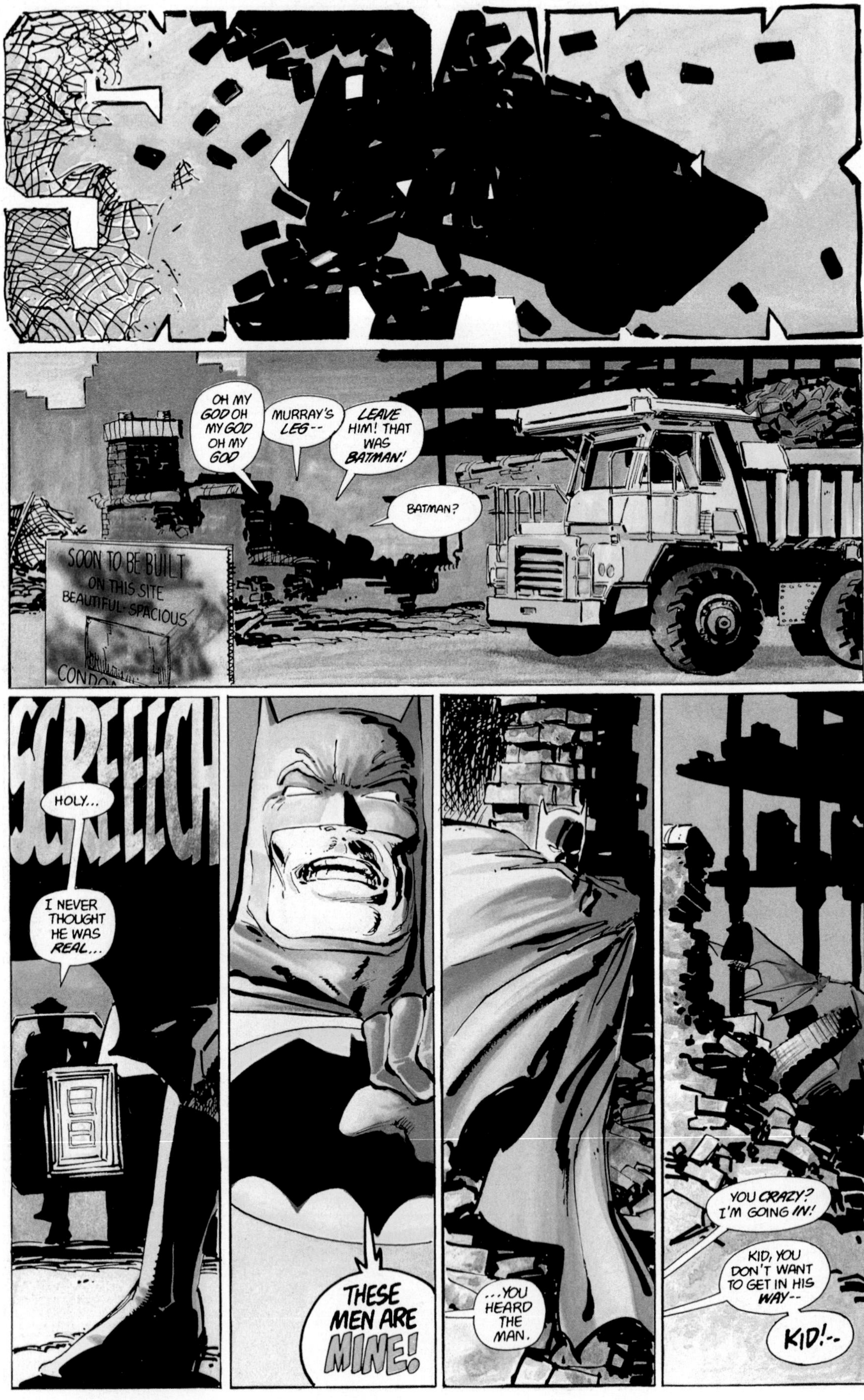
SMASH
OH MY GOD OH MY GOD OH MY GOD
MURRAY'S LEG--
LEAVE HIM! THAT WAS BATMAN!
BATMAN?
SOON TO BE BUILT ON THIS SITE BEAUTIFUL-SPACIOUS
SCREEECH
HOLY...
I NEVER THOUGHT HE WAS REAL...
THESE MEN ARE MINE!
...YOU HEARD THE MAN.
YOU CRAZY? I'M GOING IN!
KID, YOU DON'T WANT TO GET IN HIS WAY--
KID!--

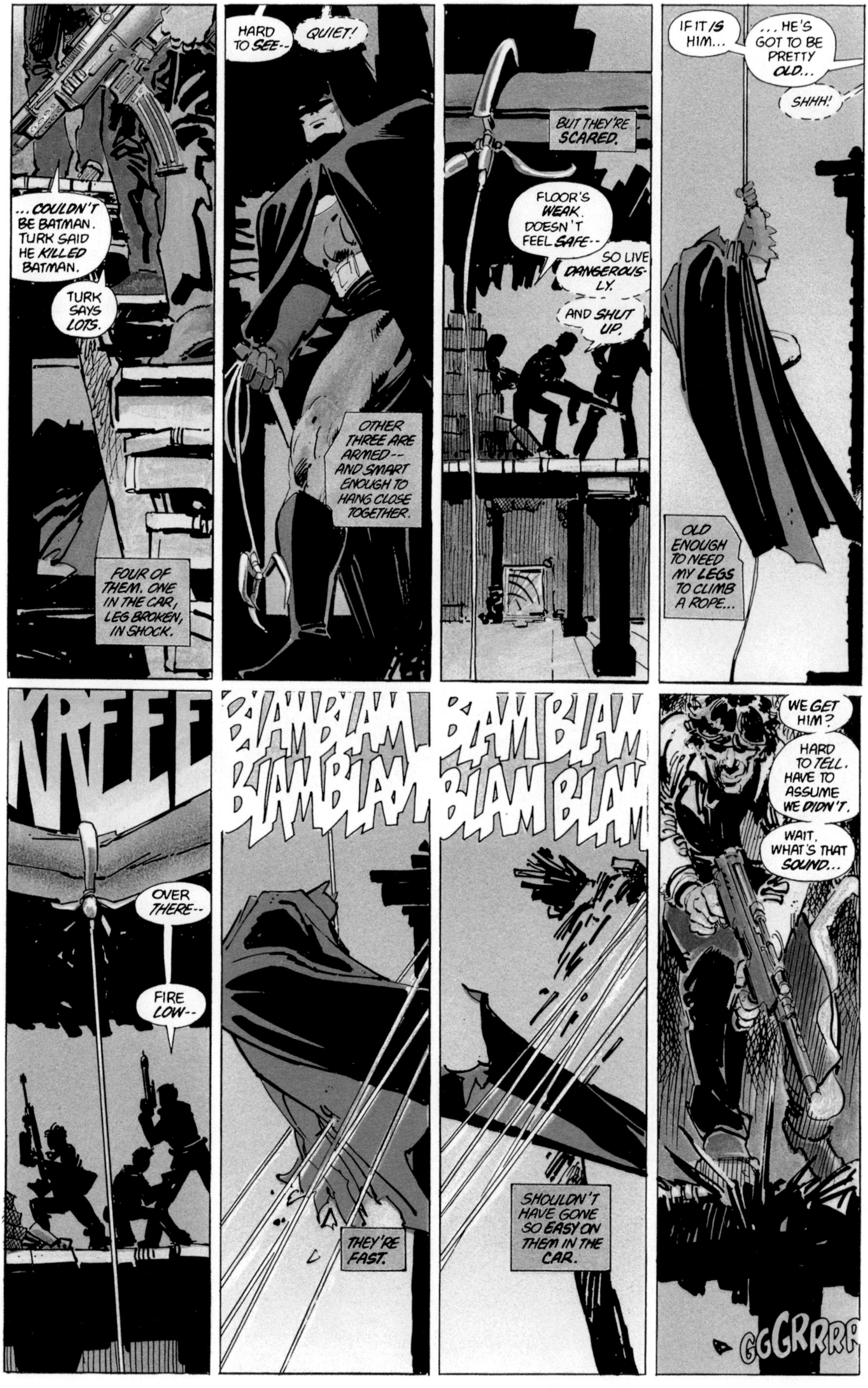
...COULDN'T BE BATMAN. TURK SAID HE KILLED BATMAN.
TURK SAYS LOTS.
FOUR OF THEM. ONE IN THE CAR, LEG BROKEN, IN SHOCK.
HARD TO SEE--
QUIET!
OTHER THREE ARE ARMED-- AND SMART ENOUGH TO HANG CLOSE TOGETHER.
BUT THEY'RE SCARED.
FLOOR'S WEAK. DOESN'T FEEL SAFE--
SO LIVE DANGEROUSLY.
AND SHUT UP.
IF IT IS HIM...
...HE'S GOT TO BE PRETTY OLD...
SHHH!
OLD ENOUGH TO NEED MY LEGS TO CLIMB A ROPE...
KREEE
OVER THERE--
FIRE LOW--
BLAM BLAM
BLAM BLAM
THEY'RE FAST.
BLAM BLAM
BLAM BLAM
SHOULDN'T HAVE GONE SO EASY ON THEM IN THE CAR.
WE GET HIM?
HARD TO TELL. HAVE TO ASSUME WE DIDN'T.
WAIT. WHAT'S THAT SOUND...
GGGRRRR

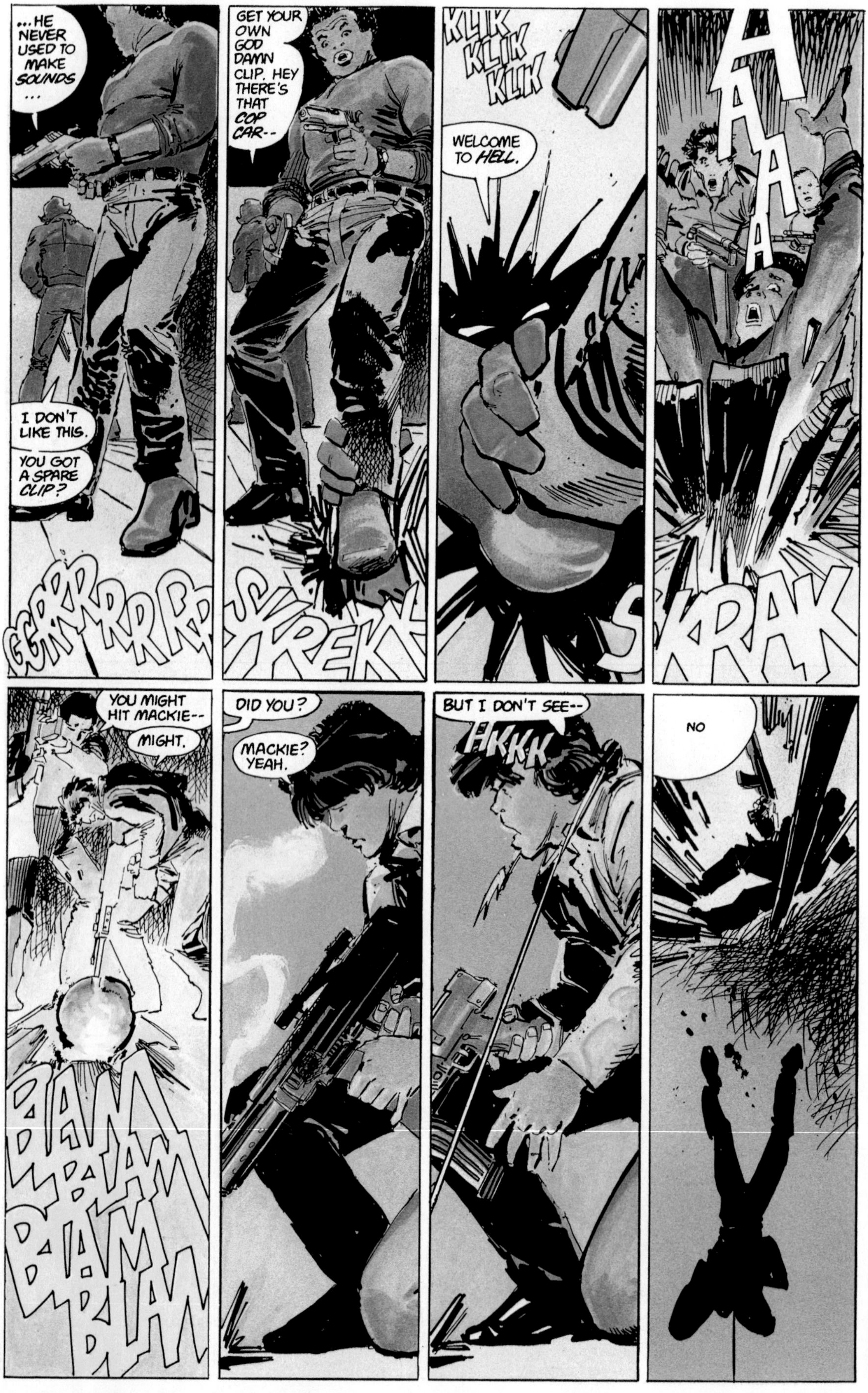
...HE NEVER USED TO MAKE SOUNDS ...
I DON'T LIKE THIS.
YOU GOT A SPARE CLIP?
GRRRRRR
GET YOUR OWN GOD DAMN CLIP. HEY THERE'S THAT COP CAR--
SKREK
KLIK KLIK KLIK
WELCOME TO HELL.
AAAAA
SKRAK
YOU MIGHT HIT MACKIE--
MIGHT.
BLAM BLAM BLAM BLAM
DID YOU?
MACKIE? YEAH.
BUT I DON'T SEE--
HKKK
NO

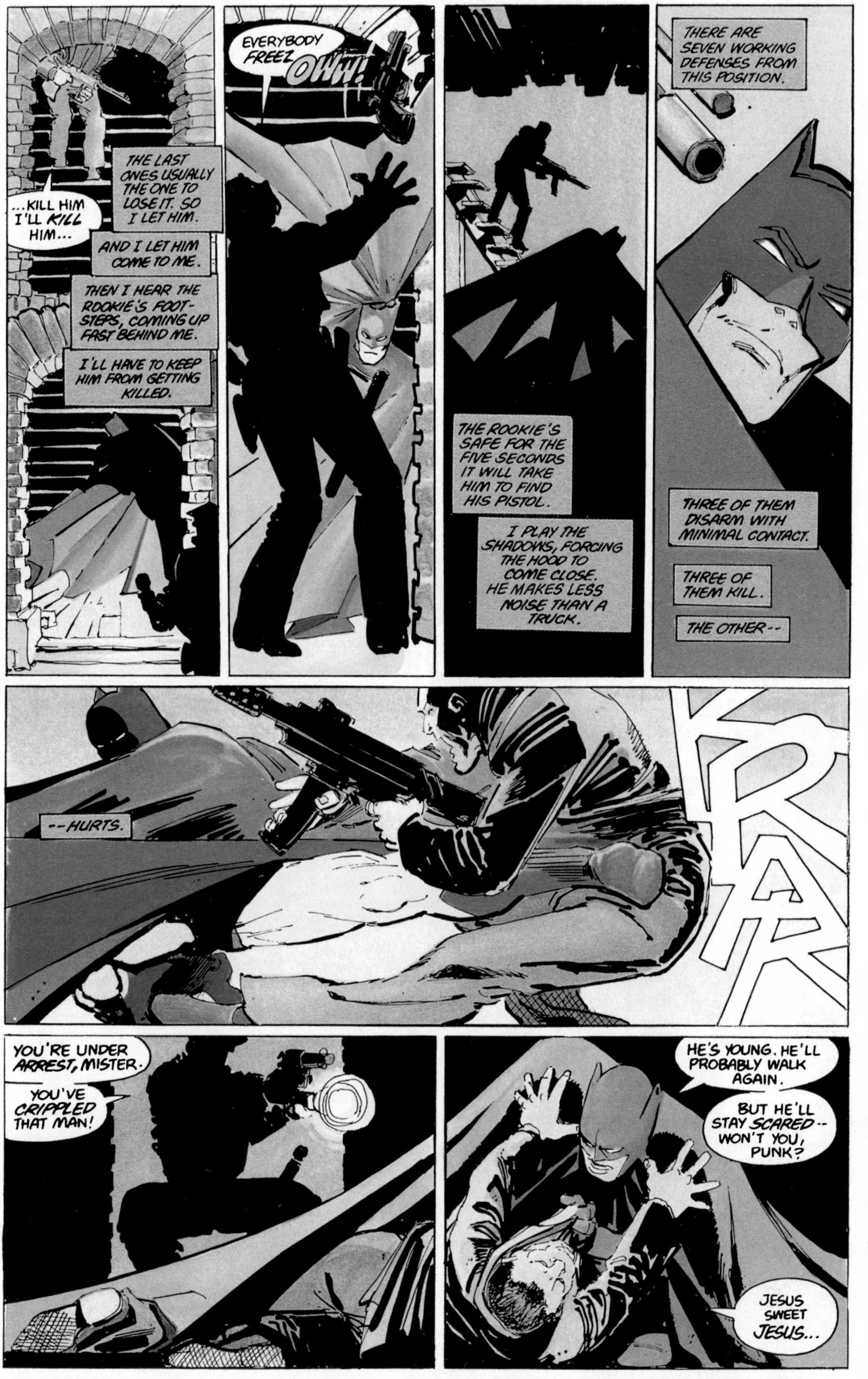
...KILL HIM I'LL KILL HIM...
THE LAST ONES USUALLY THE ONE TO LOSE IT. SO I LET HIM.
AND I LET HIM COME TO ME.
THEN I HEAR THE ROOKIE'S FOOT-STEPS, COMING UP FAST BEHIND ME.
I'LL HAVE TO KEEP HIM FROM GETTING KILLED.
EVERYBODY FREEZ
OWW!
THE ROOKIE'S SAFE FOR THE FIVE SECONDS IT WILL TAKE HIM TO FIND HIS PISTOL.
I PLAY THE SHADOWS, FORCING THE HOOD TO COME CLOSE. HE MAKES LESS NOISE THAN A TRUCK.
THERE ARE SEVEN WORKING DEFENSES FROM THIS POSITION.
THREE OF THEM DISARM WITH MINIMAL CONTACT.
THREE OF THEM KILL.
THE OTHER--
--HURTS.
KRAK
YOU'RE UNDER ARREST, MISTER.
YOU'VE CRIPPLED THAT MAN!
HE'S YOUNG. HE'LL PROBABLY WALK AGAIN.
BUT HE'LL STAY SCARED--WON'T YOU, PUNK?
JESUS SWEET JESUS...

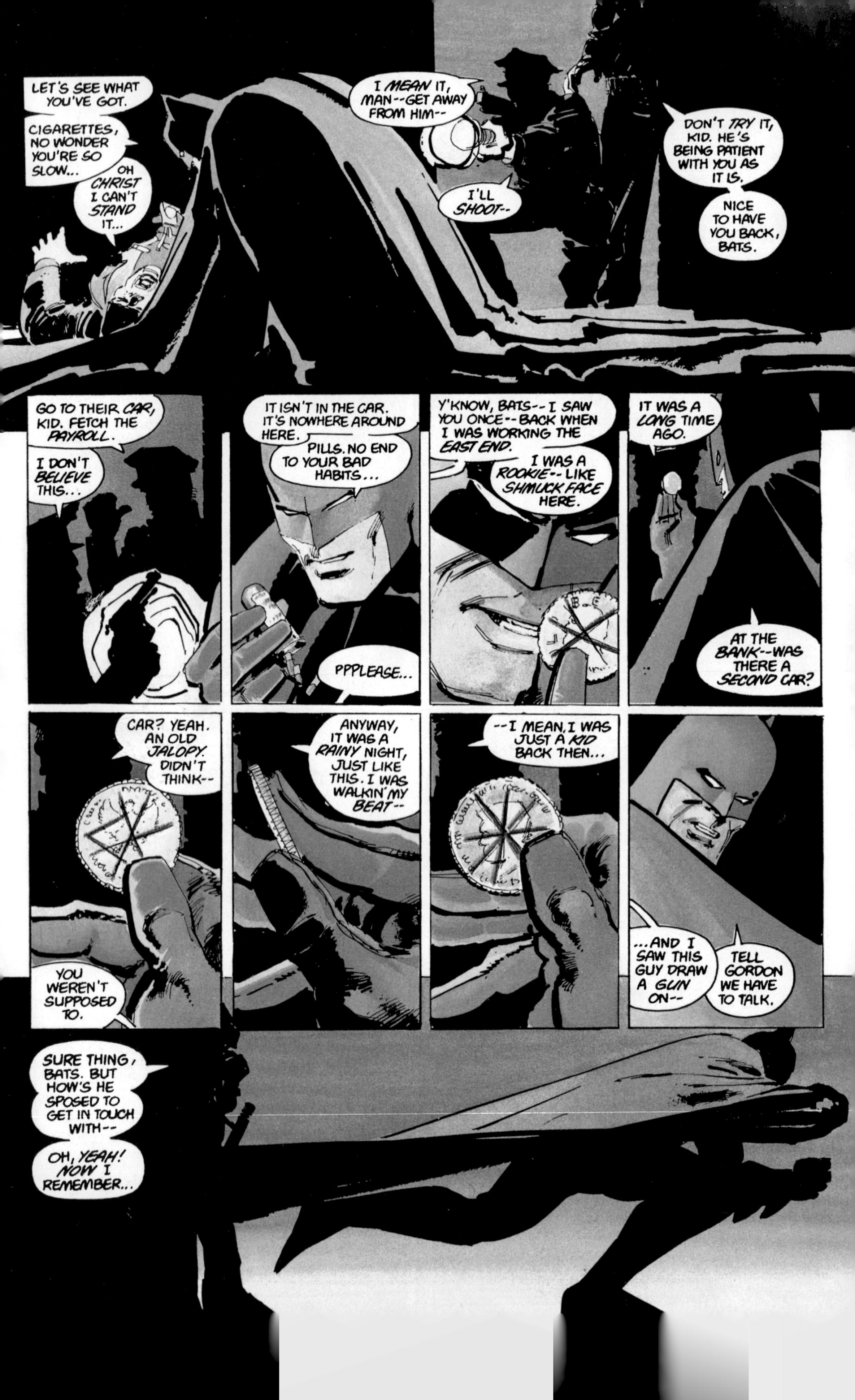
LET'S SEE WHAT YOU'VE GOT.
CIGARETTES, NO WONDER YOU'RE SO SLOW...
OH CHRIST I CAN'T STAND IT...
I MEAN IT, MAN--GET AWAY FROM HIM--
I'LL SHOOT--
DON'T TRY IT, KID. HE'S BEING PATIENT WITH YOU AS IT IS.
NICE TO HAVE YOU BACK, BATS.
GO TO THEIR CAR, KID. FETCH THE PAYROLL.
I DON'T BELIEVE THIS...
IT ISN'T IN THE CAR. IT'S NOWHERE AROUND HERE.
PILLS. NO END TO YOUR BAD HABITS...
PPPLEASE...
Y'KNOW, BATS--I SAW YOU ONCE--BACK WHEN I WAS WORKING THE EAST END.
I WAS A ROOKIE--LIKE SHMUCK FACE HERE.
IT WAS A LONG TIME AGO.
AT THE BANK--WAS THERE A SECOND CAR?
CAR? YEAH. AN OLD JALOPY. DIDN'T THINK--
YOU WEREN'T SUPPOSED TO.
ANYWAY, IT WAS A RAINY NIGHT, JUST LIKE THIS. I WAS WALKIN' MY BEAT--
--I MEAN, I WAS JUST A KID BACK THEN...
...AND I SAW THIS GUY DRAW A GUN ON--
TELL GORDON WE HAVE TO TALK.
SURE THING, BATS. BUT HOW'S HE SPOSED TO GET IN TOUCH WITH--
OH, YEAH! NOW I REMEMBER...

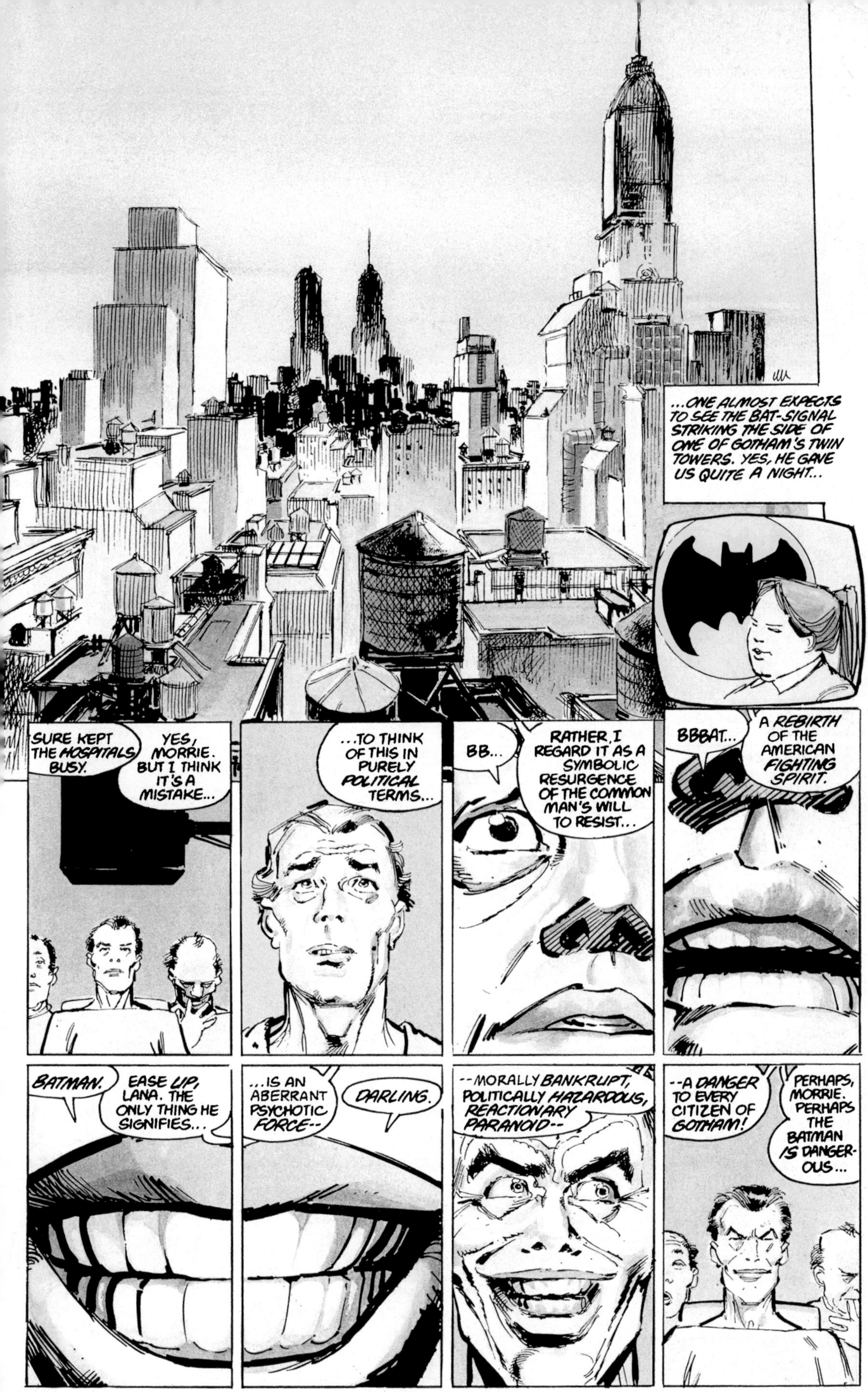

...ONE ALMOST EXPECTS TO SEE THE BAT-SIGNAL STRIKING THE SIDE OF ONE OF GOTHAM'S TWIN TOWERS. YES, HE GAVE US QUITE A NIGHT...
SURE KEPT THE HOSPITALS BUSY.
YES, MORRIE. BUT I THINK IT'S A MISTAKE...
...TO THINK OF THIS IN PURELY POLITICAL TERMS...
BB...
RATHER, I REGARD IT AS A SYMBOLIC RESURGENCE OF THE COMMON MAN'S WILL TO RESIST...
BBBAT...
A REBIRTH OF THE AMERICAN FIGHTING SPIRIT.
BATMAN.
EASE UP, LANA. THE ONLY THING HE SIGNIFIES...
...IS AN ABERRANT PSYCHOTIC FORCE--
DARLING.
--MORALLY BANKRUPT, POLITICALLY HAZARDOUS, REACTIONARY PARANOID--
--A DANGER TO EVERY CITIZEN OF GOTHAM!
PERHAPS, MORRIE. PERHAPS THE BATMAN IS DANGEROUS...

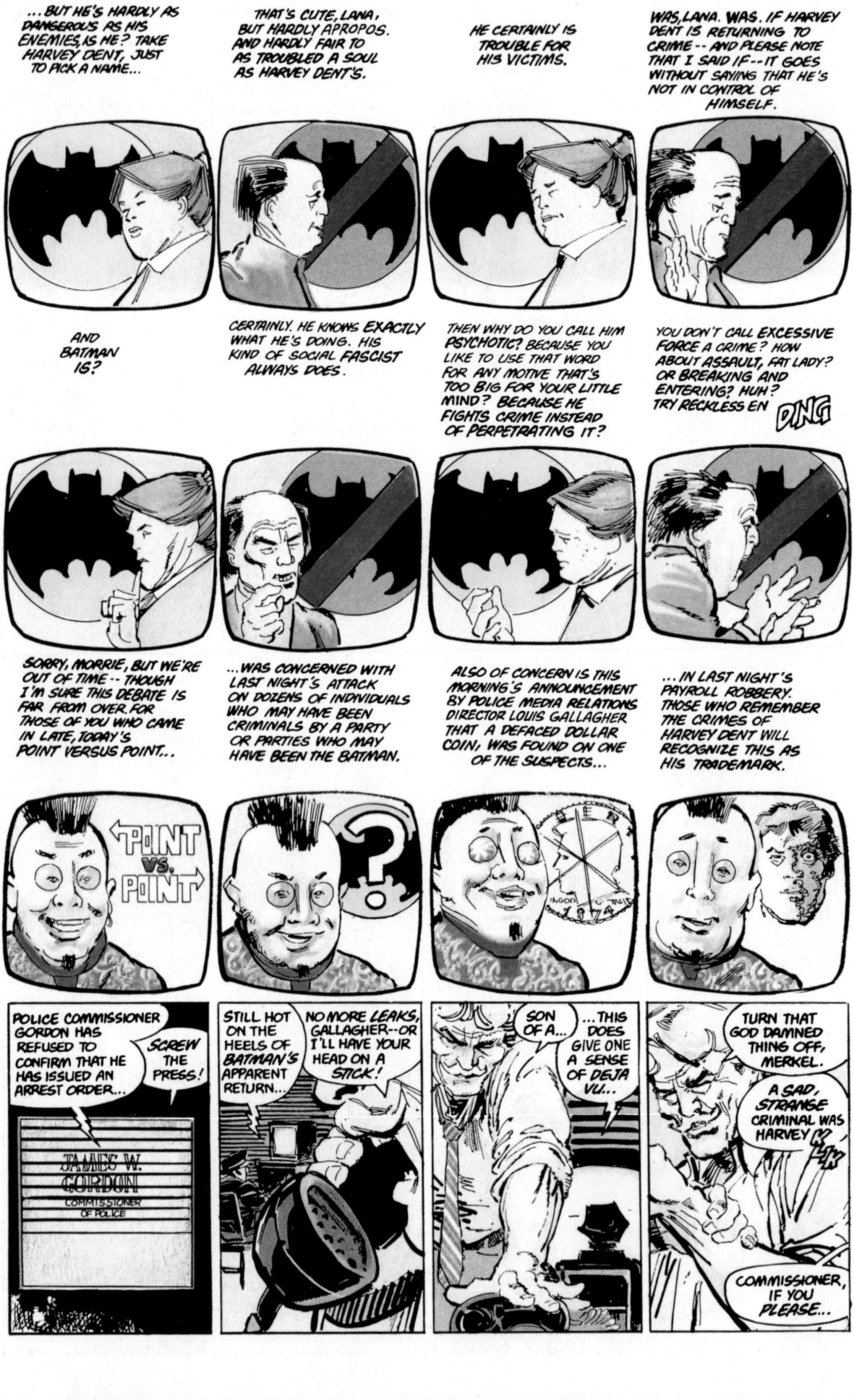

...BUT HE'S HARDLY AS DANGEROUS AS HIS ENEMIES, IS HE? TAKE HARVEY DENT, JUST TO PICK A NAME...
THAT'S CUTE, LANA, BUT HARDLY APROPOS. AND HARDLY FAIR TO AS TROUBLED A SOUL AS HARVEY DENT'S.
HE CERTAINLY IS TROUBLE FOR HIS VICTIMS.
WAS, LANA. WAS. IF HARVEY DENT IS RETURNING TO CRIME -- AND PLEASE NOTE THAT I SAID IF -- IT GOES WITHOUT SAYING THAT HE'S NOT IN CONTROL OF HIMSELF.
AND BATMAN IS?
CERTAINLY. HE KNOWS EXACTLY WHAT HE'S DOING. HIS KIND OF SOCIAL FASCIST ALWAYS DOES.
THEN WHY DO YOU CALL HIM PSYCHOTIC? BECAUSE YOU LIKE TO USE THAT WORD FOR ANY MOTIVE THAT'S TOO BIG FOR YOUR LITTLE MIND? BECAUSE HE FIGHTS CRIME INSTEAD OF PERPETRATING IT?
YOU DON'T CALL EXCESSIVE FORCE A CRIME? HOW ABOUT ASSAULT, FAT LADY? OR BREAKING AND ENTERING? HUH? TRY RECKLESS EN
DING
SORRY, MORRIE, BUT WE'RE OUT OF TIME -- THOUGH I'M SURE THIS DEBATE IS FAR FROM OVER. FOR THOSE OF YOU WHO CAME IN LATE, TODAY'S POINT VERSUS POINT...
POINT vs. POINT
...WAS CONCERNED WITH LAST NIGHT'S ATTACK ON DOZENS OF INDIVIDUALS WHO MAY HAVE BEEN CRIMINALS BY A PARTY OR PARTIES WHO MAY HAVE BEEN THE BATMAN.
ALSO OF CONCERN IS THIS MORNING'S ANNOUNCEMENT BY POLICE MEDIA RELATIONS DIRECTOR LOUIS GALLAGHER THAT A DEFACED DOLLAR COIN, WAS FOUND ON ONE OF THE SUSPECTS...
...IN LAST NIGHT'S PAYROLL ROBBERY. THOSE WHO REMEMBER THE CRIMES OF HARVEY DENT WILL RECOGNIZE THIS AS HIS TRADEMARK.
POLICE COMMISSIONER GORDON HAS REFUSED TO CONFIRM THAT HE HAS ISSUED AN ARREST ORDER...
SCREW THE PRESS!
JAMES W. GORDON COMMISSIONER OF POLICE
STILL HOT ON THE HEELS OF BATMAN'S APPARENT RETURN...
NO MORE LEAKS, GALLAGHER--OR I'LL HAVE YOUR HEAD ON A STICK!
SON OF A...
...THIS DOES GIVE ONE A SENSE OF DEJA VU...
TURN THAT GOD DAMNED THING OFF, MERKEL.
A SAD, STRANGE CRIMINAL WAS HARVEY
KLIK
COMMISSIONER, IF YOU PLEASE...

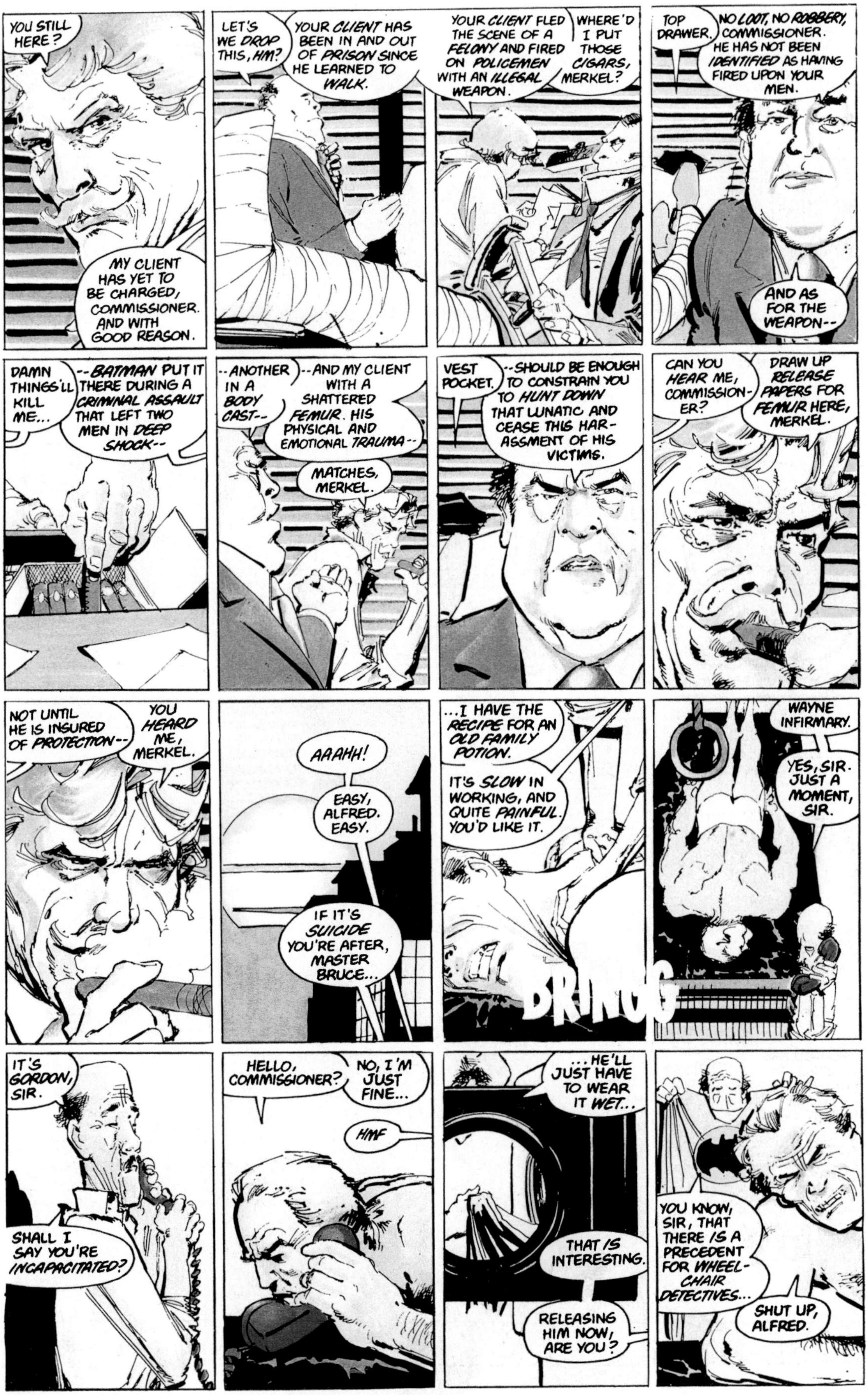
YOU STILL HERE?
MY CLIENT HAS YET TO BE CHARGED, COMMISSIONER. AND WITH GOOD REASON.
LET'S WE DROP THIS, HM?
YOUR CLIENT HAS BEEN IN AND OUT OF PRISON SINCE HE LEARNED TO WALK.
YOUR CLIENT FLED THE SCENE OF A FELONY AND FIRED ON POLICEMEN WITH AN ILLEGAL WEAPON.
WHERE'D I PUT THOSE CIGARS, MERKEL?
TOP DRAWER.
NO LOOT, NO ROBBERY, COMMISSIONER. HE HAS NOT BEEN IDENTIFIED AS HAVING FIRED UPON YOUR MEN.
AND AS FOR THE WEAPON--
DAMN THINGS'LL KILL ME...
--BATMAN PUT IT THERE DURING A CRIMINAL ASSAULT THAT LEFT TWO MEN IN DEEP SHOCK--
--ANOTHER IN A BODY CAST--
--AND MY CLIENT WITH A SHATTERED FEMUR. HIS PHYSICAL AND EMOTIONAL TRAUMA--
MATCHES, MERKEL.
VEST POCKET.
--SHOULD BE ENOUGH TO CONSTRAIN YOU TO HUNT DOWN THAT LUNATIC AND CEASE THIS HARASSMENT OF HIS VICTIMS.
CAN YOU HEAR ME, COMMISSIONER?
DRAW UP RELEASE PAPERS FOR FEMUR HERE, MERKEL.
NOT UNTIL HE IS INSURED OF PROTECTION--
YOU HEARD ME, MERKEL.
AAAHH!
EASY, ALFRED. EASY.
IF IT'S SUICIDE YOU'RE AFTER, MASTER BRUCE...
...I HAVE THE RECIPE FOR AN OLD FAMILY POTION.
IT'S SLOW IN WORKING, AND QUITE PAINFUL. YOU'D LIKE IT.
BRINNG
WAYNE INFIRMARY.
YES, SIR. JUST A MOMENT, SIR.
IT'S GORDON, SIR.
SHALL I SAY YOU'RE INCAPACITATED?
HELLO, COMMISSIONER?
NO, I'M JUST FINE...
HMF
...HE'LL JUST HAVE TO WEAR IT WET...
THAT IS INTERESTING.
RELEASING HIM NOW, ARE YOU?
YOU KNOW, SIR, THAT THERE IS A PRECEDENT FOR WHEELCHAIR DETECTIVES...
SHUT UP, ALFRED.

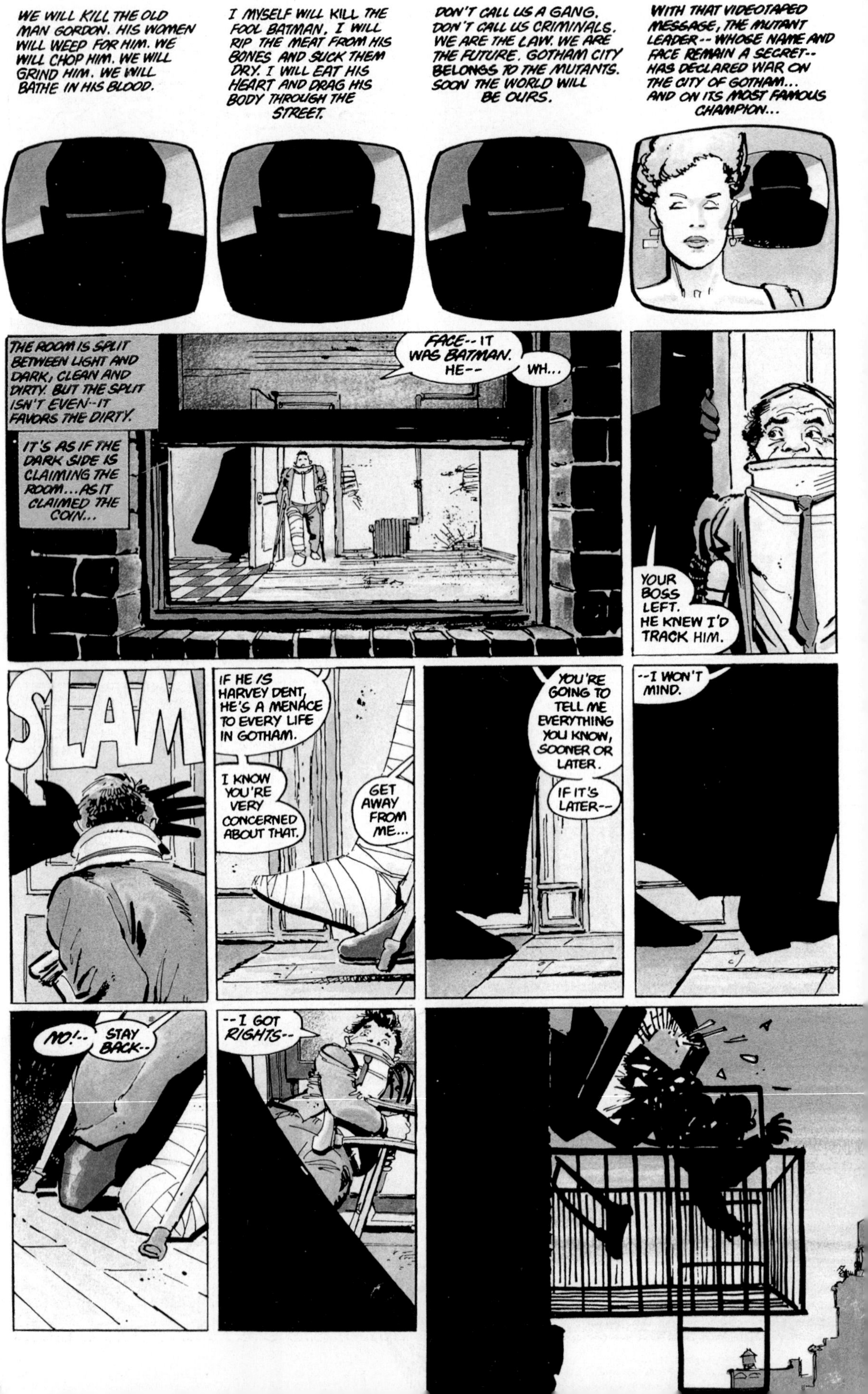
WE WILL KILL THE OLD MAN GORDON. HIS WOMEN WILL WEEP FOR HIM. WE WILL CHOP HIM. WE WILL GRIND HIM. WE WILL BATHE IN HIS BLOOD.
I MYSELF WILL KILL THE FOOL BATMAN. I WILL RIP THE MEAT FROM HIS BONES AND SUCK THEM DRY. I WILL EAT HIS HEART AND DRAG HIS BODY THROUGH THE STREET.
DON'T CALL US A GANG. DON'T CALL US CRIMINALS. WE ARE THE LAW. WE ARE THE FUTURE. GOTHAM CITY BELONGS TO THE MUTANTS. SOON THE WORLD WILL BE OURS.
WITH THAT VIDEOTAPED MESSAGE, THE MUTANT LEADER-- WHOSE NAME AND FACE REMAIN A SECRET-- HAS DECLARED WAR ON THE CITY OF GOTHAM... AND ON ITS MOST FAMOUS CHAMPION...
THE ROOM IS SPLIT BETWEEN LIGHT AND DARK, CLEAN AND DIRTY. BUT THE SPLIT ISN'T EVEN--IT FAVORS THE DIRTY.
IT'S AS IF THE DARK SIDE IS CLAIMING THE ROOM...AS IT CLAIMED THE COIN...
FACE-- IT WAS BATMAN. HE--
WH...
YOUR BOSS LEFT. HE KNEW I'D TRACK HIM.
SLAM
IF HE IS HARVEY DENT, HE'S A MENACE TO EVERY LIFE IN GOTHAM.
I KNOW YOU'RE VERY CONCERNED ABOUT THAT.
GET AWAY FROM ME...
YOU'RE GOING TO TELL ME EVERYTHING YOU KNOW, SOONER OR LATER.
IF IT'S LATER--
--I WON'T MIND.
NO!--
STAY BACK--
--I GOT RIGHTS--

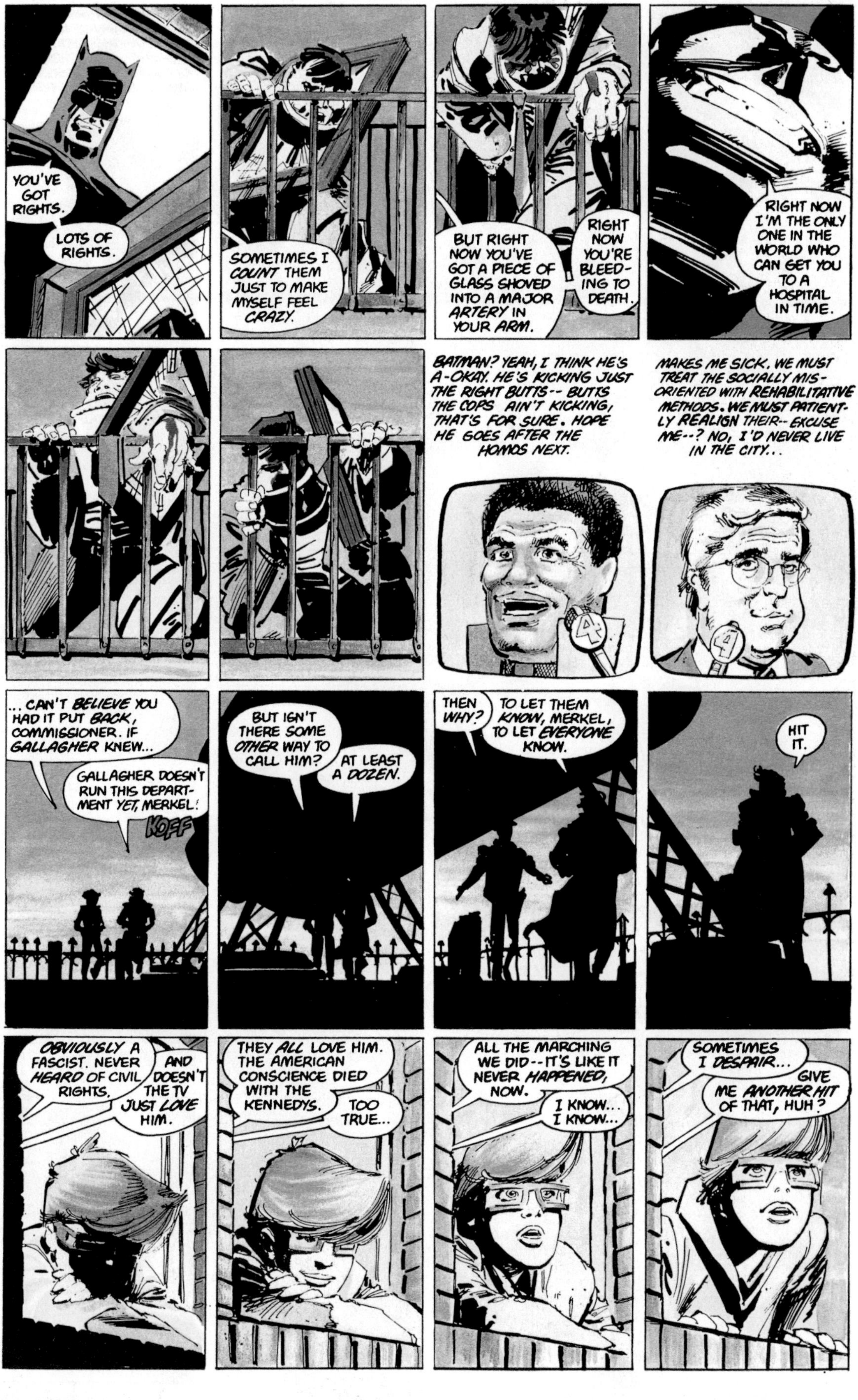

YOU'VE GOT RIGHTS.
LOTS OF RIGHTS.
SOMETIMES I COUNT THEM JUST TO MAKE MYSELF FEEL CRAZY.
BUT RIGHT NOW YOU'VE GOT A PIECE OF GLASS SHOVED INTO A MAJOR ARTERY IN YOUR ARM.
RIGHT NOW YOU'RE BLEEDING TO DEATH.
RIGHT NOW I'M THE ONLY ONE IN THE WORLD WHO CAN GET YOU TO A HOSPITAL IN TIME.
BATMAN? YEAH, I THINK HE'S A-OKAY. HE'S KICKING JUST THE RIGHT BUTTS -- BUTTS THE COPS AIN'T KICKING, THAT'S FOR SURE. HOPE HE GOES AFTER THE HOMOS NEXT.
MAKES ME SICK. WE MUST TREAT THE SOCIALLY MIS-ORIENTED WITH REHABILITATIVE METHODS. WE MUST PATIENTLY REALIGN THEIR-- EXCUSE ME--? NO, I'D NEVER LIVE IN THE CITY...
... CAN'T BELIEVE YOU HAD IT PUT BACK, COMMISSIONER. IF GALLAGHER KNEW...
GALLAGHER DOESN'T RUN THIS DEPARTMENT YET, MERKEL!
KOFF
BUT ISN'T THERE SOME OTHER WAY TO CALL HIM?
AT LEAST A DOZEN.
THEN WHY?
TO LET THEM KNOW, MERKEL, TO LET EVERYONE KNOW.
HIT IT.
OBVIOUSLY A FASCIST. NEVER HEARD OF CIVIL RIGHTS.
AND DOESN'T THE TV JUST LOVE HIM.
THEY ALL LOVE HIM. THE AMERICAN CONSCIENCE DIED WITH THE KENNEDYS.
TOO TRUE...
ALL THE MARCHING WE DID--IT'S LIKE IT NEVER HAPPENED, NOW.
I KNOW... I KNOW...
SOMETIMES I DESPAIR...
GIVE ME ANOTHER HIT OF THAT, HUH?

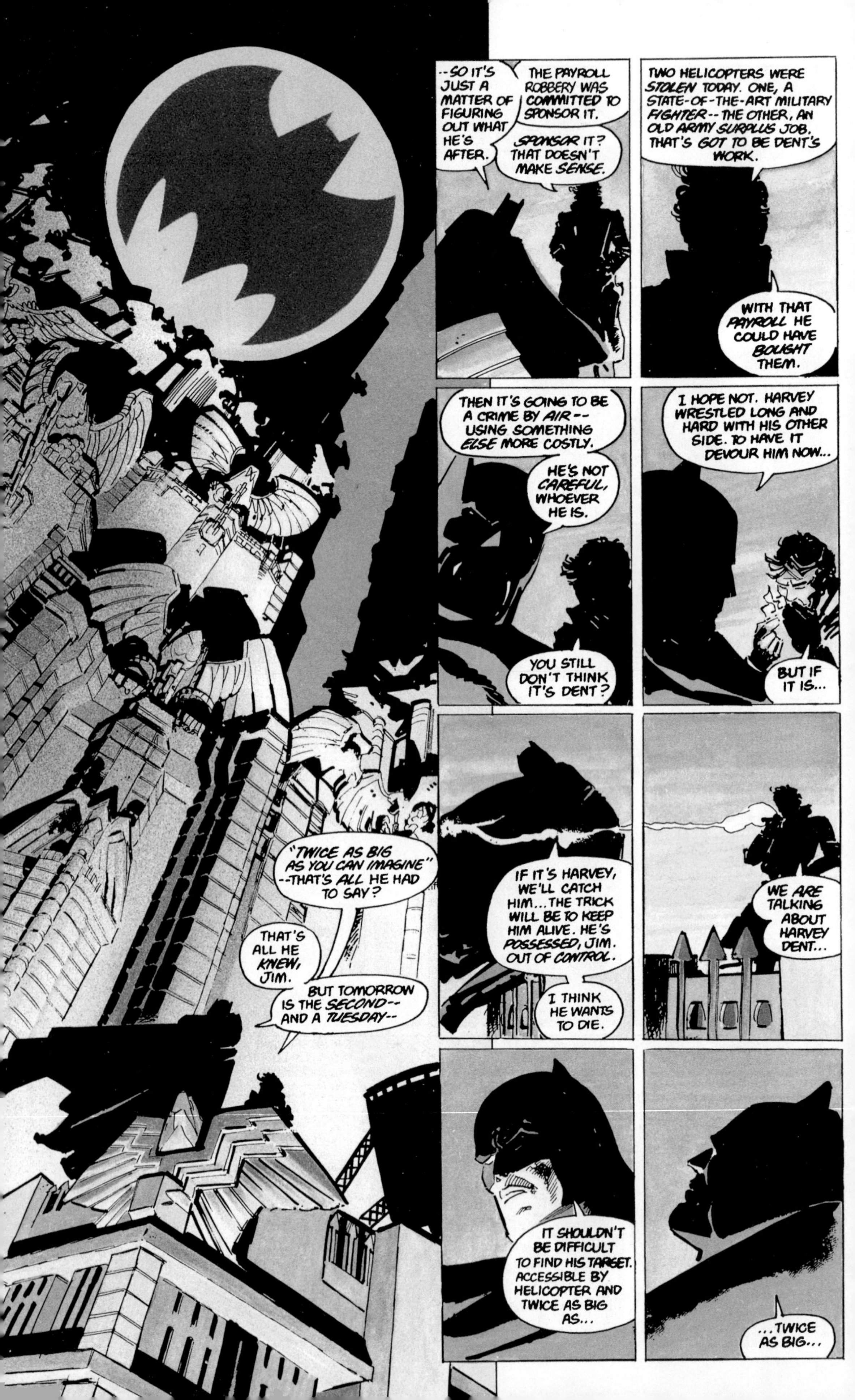
--SO IT'S JUST A MATTER OF FIGURING OUT WHAT HE'S AFTER.
THE PAYROLL ROBBERY WAS COMMITTED TO SPONSOR IT.
SPONSOR IT? THAT DOESN'T MAKE SENSE.
TWO HELICOPTERS WERE STOLEN TODAY. ONE, A STATE-OF-THE-ART MILITARY FIGHTER--THE OTHER, AN OLD ARMY SURPLUS JOB. THAT'S GOT TO BE DENT'S WORK.
WITH THAT PAYROLL HE COULD HAVE BOUGHT THEM.
THEN IT'S GOING TO BE A CRIME BY AIR-- USING SOMETHING ELSE MORE COSTLY.
HE'S NOT CAREFUL, WHOEVER HE IS.
YOU STILL DON'T THINK IT'S DENT?
I HOPE NOT. HARVEY WRESTLED LONG AND HARD WITH HIS OTHER SIDE. TO HAVE IT DEVOUR HIM NOW...
BUT IF IT IS...
IF IT'S HARVEY, WE'LL CATCH HIM...THE TRICK WILL BE TO KEEP HIM ALIVE. HE'S POSSESSED, JIM. OUT OF CONTROL.
I THINK HE WANTS TO DIE.
WE ARE TALKING ABOUT HARVEY DENT...
"TWICE AS BIG AS YOU CAN IMAGINE" --THAT'S ALL HE HAD TO SAY?
THAT'S ALL HE KNEW, JIM.
BUT TOMORROW IS THE SECOND-- AND A TUESDAY--
IT SHOULDN'T BE DIFFICULT TO FIND HIS TARGET. ACCESSIBLE BY HELICOPTER AND TWICE AS BIG AS...
...TWICE AS BIG...

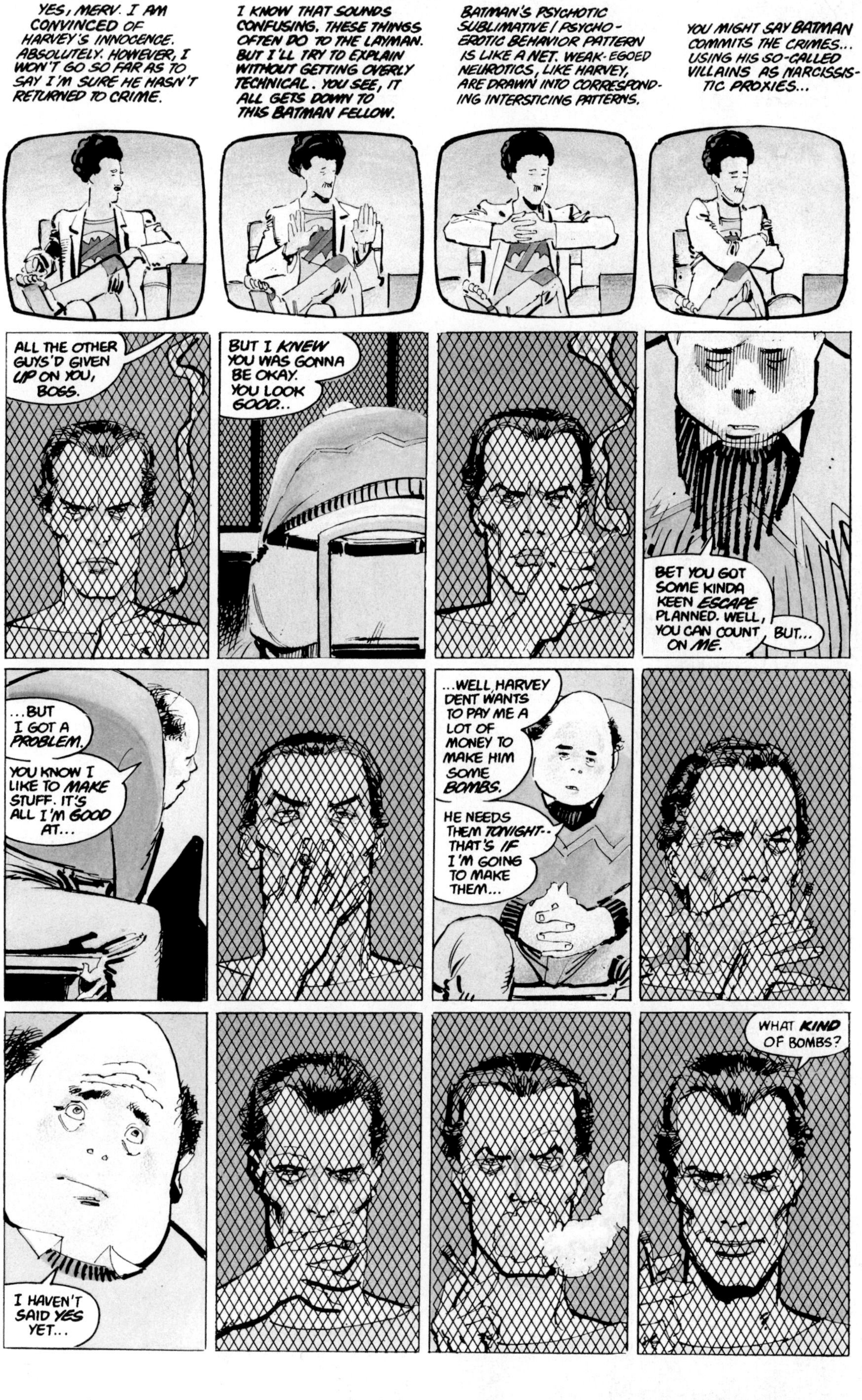

YES, MERV. I AM CONVINCED OF HARVEY'S INNOCENCE. ABSOLUTELY. HOWEVER, I WON'T GO SO FAR AS TO SAY I'M SURE HE HASN'T RETURNED TO CRIME.
I KNOW THAT SOUNDS CONFUSING. THESE THINGS OFTEN DO TO THE LAYMAN. BUT I'LL TRY TO EXPLAIN WITHOUT GETTING OVERLY TECHNICAL. YOU SEE, IT ALL GETS DOWN TO THIS BATMAN FELLOW.
BATMAN'S PSYCHOTIC SUBLIMATIVE / PSYCHO-EROTIC BEHAVIOR PATTERN IS LIKE A NET. WEAK-EGOED NEUROTICS, LIKE HARVEY, ARE DRAWN INTO CORRESPONDING INTERSTICING PATTERNS.
YOU MIGHT SAY BATMAN COMMITS THE CRIMES... USING HIS SO-CALLED VILLAINS AS NARCISSISTIC PROXIES...
ALL THE OTHER GUYS'D GIVEN UP ON YOU, BOSS.
BUT I KNEW YOU WAS GONNA BE OKAY. YOU LOOK GOOD...
BET YOU GOT SOME KINDA KEEN ESCAPE PLANNED. WELL, YOU CAN COUNT ON ME.
BUT...
...BUT I GOT A PROBLEM.
YOU KNOW I LIKE TO MAKE STUFF. IT'S ALL I'M GOOD AT...
...WELL, HARVEY DENT WANTS TO PAY ME A LOT OF MONEY TO MAKE HIM SOME BOMBS.
HE NEEDS THEM TONIGHT-- THAT'S IF I'M GOING TO MAKE THEM...
I HAVEN'T SAID YES YET...
WHAT KIND OF BOMBS?

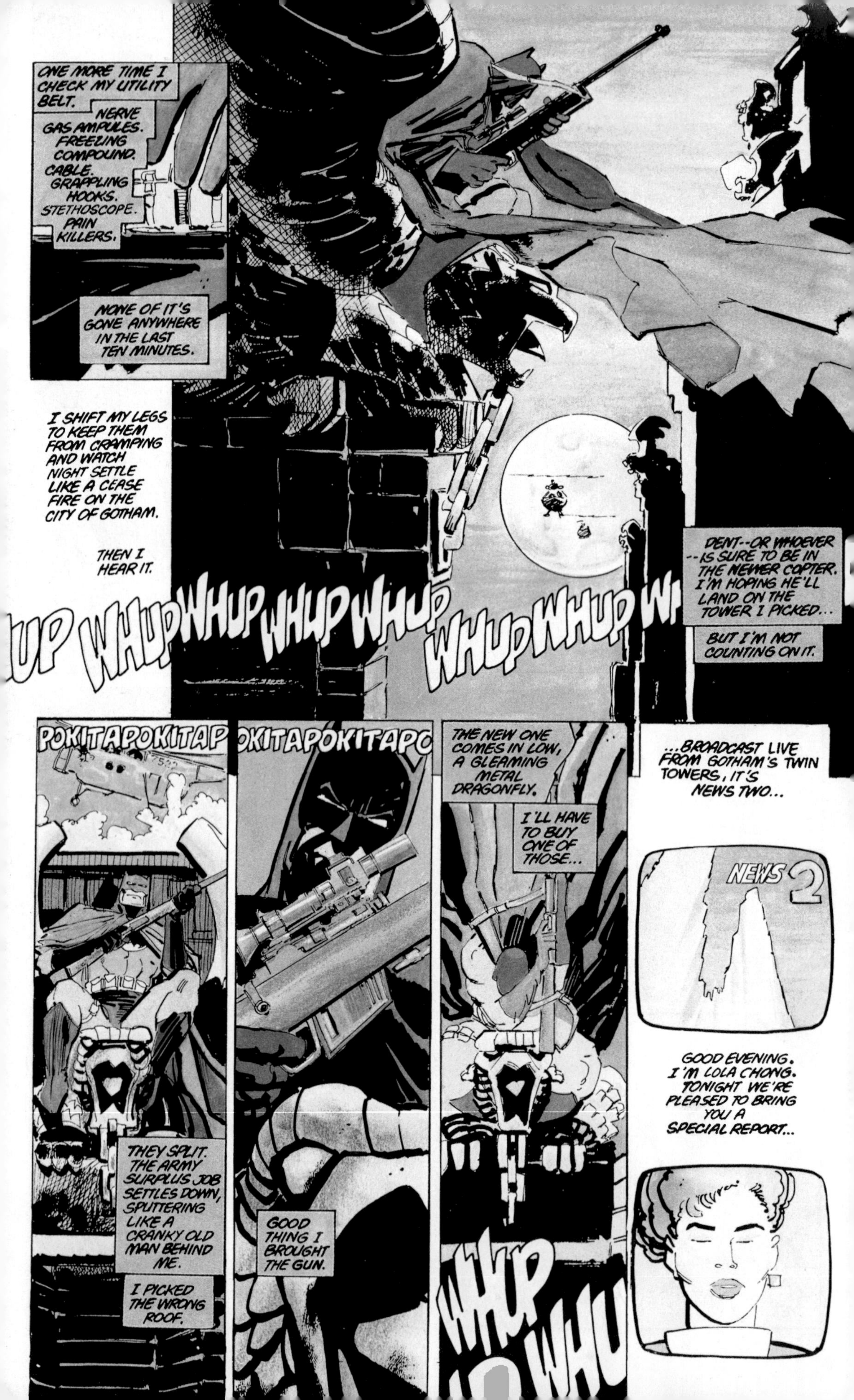
ONE MORE TIME I CHECK MY UTILITY BELT.
NERVE GAS AMPULES. FREEZING COMPOUND. CABLE. GRAPPLING HOOKS. STETHOSCOPE. PAIN KILLERS.
NONE OF IT'S GONE ANYWHERE IN THE LAST TEN MINUTES.
I SHIFT MY LEGS TO KEEP THEM FROM CRAMPING AND WATCH NIGHT SETTLE LIKE A CEASE FIRE ON THE CITY OF GOTHAM.
THEN I HEAR IT.
UP WHUP WHUP WHUP WHUP WHUP WHUP
DENT--OR WHOEVER--IS SURE TO BE IN THE NEWER COPTER. I'M HOPING HE'LL LAND ON THE TOWER I PICKED...
BUT I'M NOT COUNTING ON IT.
POKITAPOKITAP
OKITAPOKITAPO
THEY SPLIT. THE ARMY SURPLUS JOB SETTLES DOWN, SPUTTERING LIKE A CRANKY OLD MAN BEHIND ME.
I PICKED THE WRONG ROOF.
GOOD THING I BROUGHT THE GUN.
THE NEW ONE COMES IN LOW, A GLEAMING METAL DRAGONFLY.
I'LL HAVE TO BUY ONE OF THOSE...
WHUP WHU
...BROADCAST LIVE FROM GOTHAM'S TWIN TOWERS, IT'S NEWS TWO...
NEWS 2
GOOD EVENING. I'M LOLA CHONG. TONIGHT WE'RE PLEASED TO BRING YOU A SPECIAL REPORT...

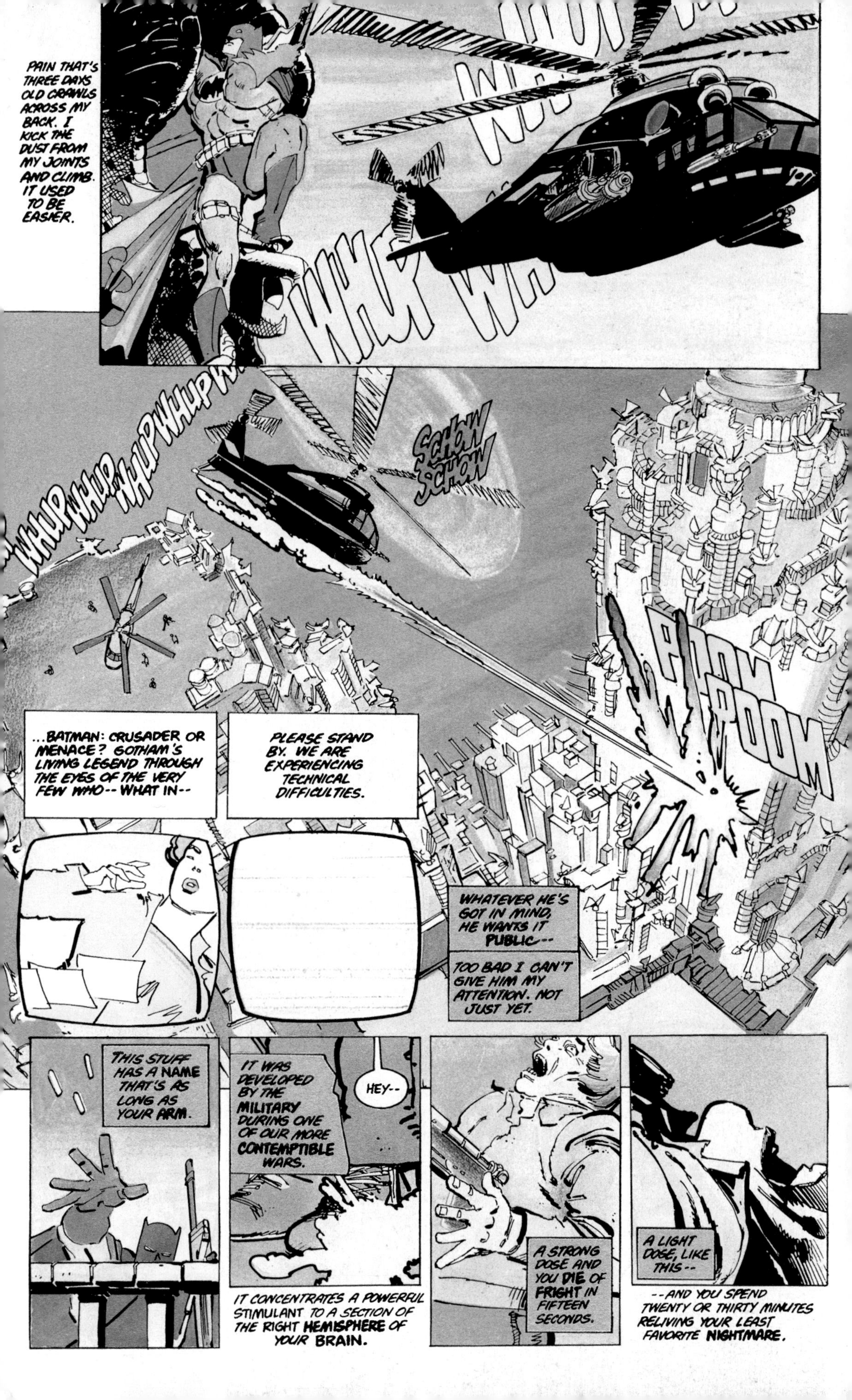
PAIN THAT'S THREE DAYS OLD CRAWLS ACROSS MY BACK. I KICK THE DUST FROM MY JOINTS AND CLIMB. IT USED TO BE EASIER.
WHUP
WHUP WHUP WHUP WHUP
SCHOW SCHOW
POOM POOM
...BATMAN: CRUSADER OR MENACE? GOTHAM'S LIVING LEGEND THROUGH THE EYES OF THE VERY FEW WHO-- WHAT IN--
PLEASE STAND BY. WE ARE EXPERIENCING TECHNICAL DIFFICULTIES.
WHATEVER HE'S GOT IN MIND, HE WANTS IT PUBLIC--
TOO BAD I CAN'T GIVE HIM MY ATTENTION. NOT JUST YET.
THIS STUFF HAS A NAME THAT'S AS LONG AS YOUR ARM.
IT WAS DEVELOPED BY THE MILITARY DURING ONE OF OUR MORE CONTEMPTIBLE WARS.
HEY--
IT CONCENTRATES A POWERFUL STIMULANT TO A SECTION OF THE RIGHT HEMISPHERE OF YOUR BRAIN.
A STRONG DOSE AND YOU DIE OF FRIGHT IN FIFTEEN SECONDS.
A LIGHT DOSE, LIKE THIS--
--AND YOU SPEND TWENTY OR THIRTY MINUTES RELIVING YOUR LEAST FAVORITE NIGHTMARE.

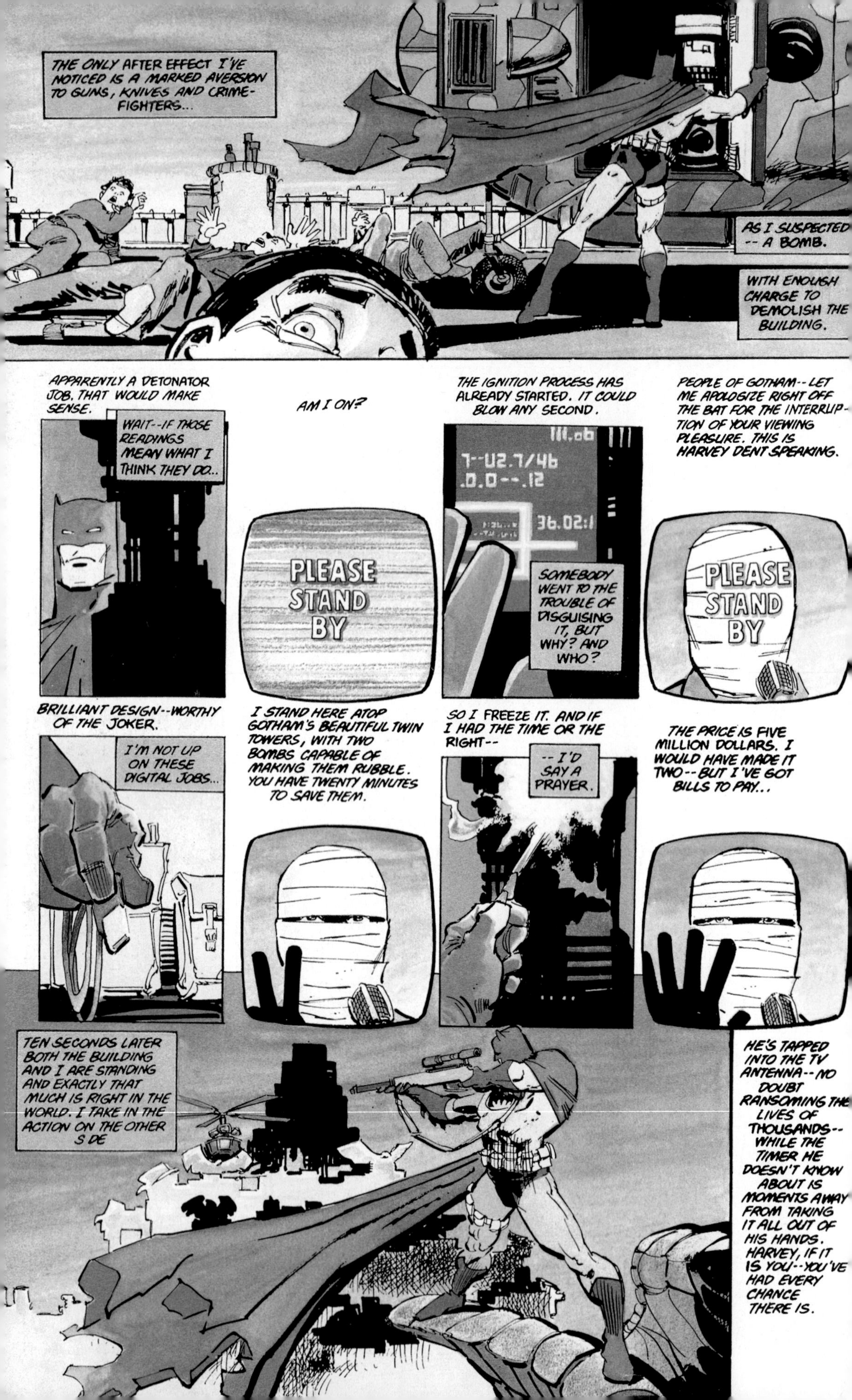

THE ONLY AFTER EFFECT I'VE NOTICED IS A MARKED AVERSION TO GUNS, KNIVES AND CRIME-FIGHTERS...
AS I SUSPECTED -- A BOMB.
WITH ENOUGH CHARGE TO DEMOLISH THE BUILDING.
APPARENTLY A DETONATOR JOB. THAT WOULD MAKE SENSE.
WAIT--IF THOSE READINGS MEAN WHAT I THINK THEY DO...
AM I ON?
PLEASE STAND BY
THE IGNITION PROCESS HAS ALREADY STARTED. IT COULD BLOW ANY SECOND.
SOMEBODY WENT TO THE TROUBLE OF DISGUISING IT, BUT WHY? AND WHO?
PEOPLE OF GOTHAM--LET ME APOLOGIZE RIGHT OFF THE BAT FOR THE INTERRUPTION OF YOUR VIEWING PLEASURE. THIS IS HARVEY DENT SPEAKING.
PLEASE STAND BY
BRILLIANT DESIGN--WORTHY OF THE JOKER.
I'M NOT UP ON THESE DIGITAL JOBS...
I STAND HERE ATOP GOTHAM'S BEAUTIFUL TWIN TOWERS, WITH TWO BOMBS CAPABLE OF MAKING THEM RUBBLE. YOU HAVE TWENTY MINUTES TO SAVE THEM.
SO I FREEZE IT. AND IF I HAD THE TIME OR THE RIGHT--
--I'D SAY A PRAYER.
THE PRICE IS FIVE MILLION DOLLARS. I WOULD HAVE MADE IT TWO--BUT I'VE GOT BILLS TO PAY...
TEN SECONDS LATER BOTH THE BUILDING AND I ARE STANDING AND EXACTLY THAT MUCH IS RIGHT IN THE WORLD. I TAKE IN THE ACTION ON THE OTHER S DE
HE'S TAPPED INTO THE TV ANTENNA--NO DOUBT RANSOMING THE LIVES OF THOUSANDS--WHILE THE TIMER HE DOESN'T KNOW ABOUT IS MOMENTS AWAY FROM TAKING IT ALL OUT OF HIS HANDS. HARVEY, IF IT IS YOU--YOU'VE HAD EVERY CHANCE THERE IS.

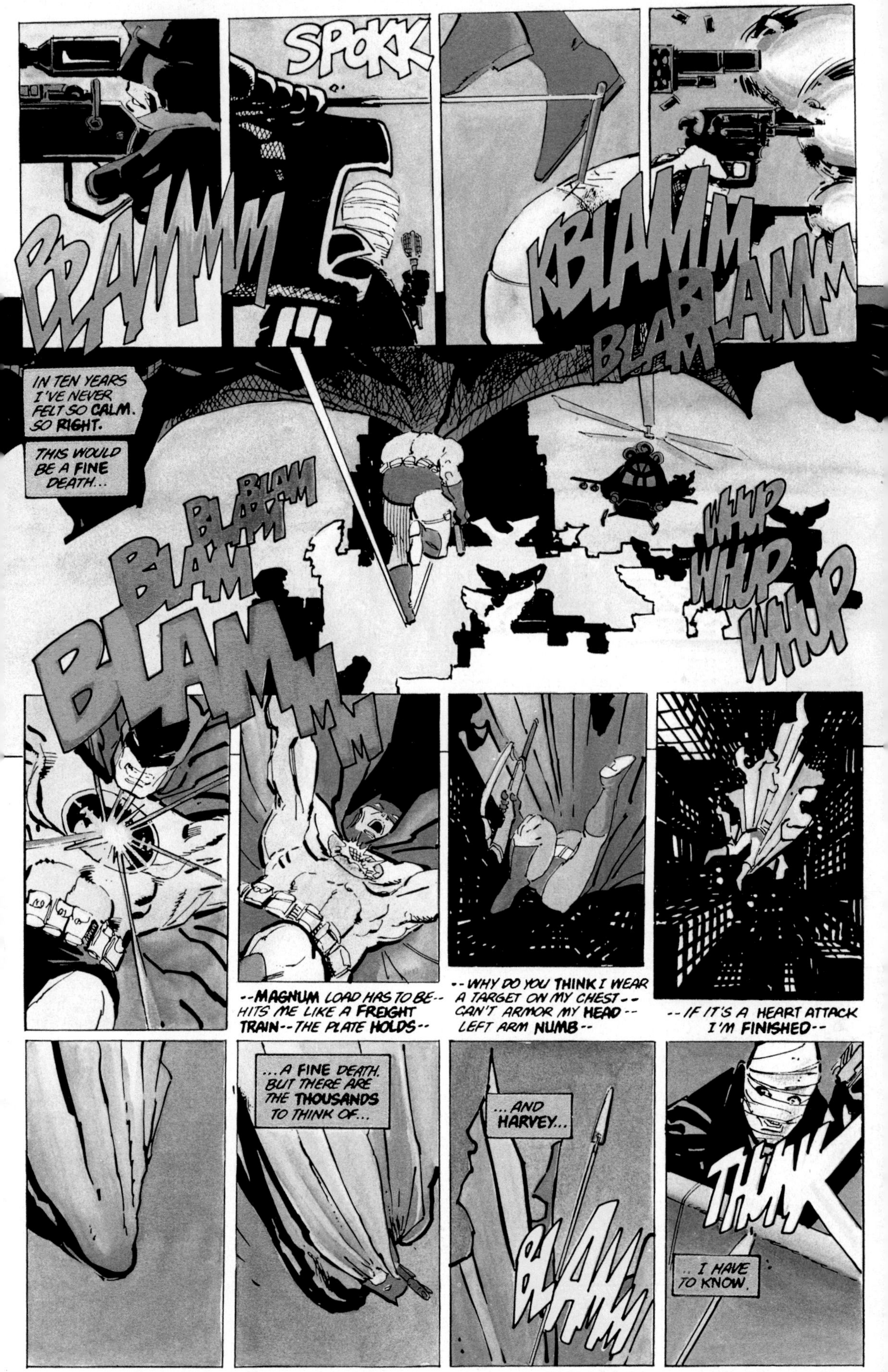

SPOKK
BRAMMM
KBLAMM
BLAM
BLAMM
IN TEN YEARS I'VE NEVER FELT SO CALM. SO RIGHT.
THIS WOULD BE A FINE DEATH...
BLAM
BLAM
BLAM
BLAMMM
WHUP
WHUP
WHUP
--MAGNUM LOAD HAS TO BE-- HITS ME LIKE A FREIGHT TRAIN--THE PLATE HOLDS--
--WHY DO YOU THINK I WEAR A TARGET ON MY CHEST-- CAN'T ARMOR MY HEAD-- LEFT ARM NUMB--
--IF IT'S A HEART ATTACK I'M FINISHED--
...A FINE DEATH. BUT THERE ARE THE THOUSANDS TO THINK OF...
...AND HARVEY...
BLAMM
THUK
...I HAVE TO KNOW.

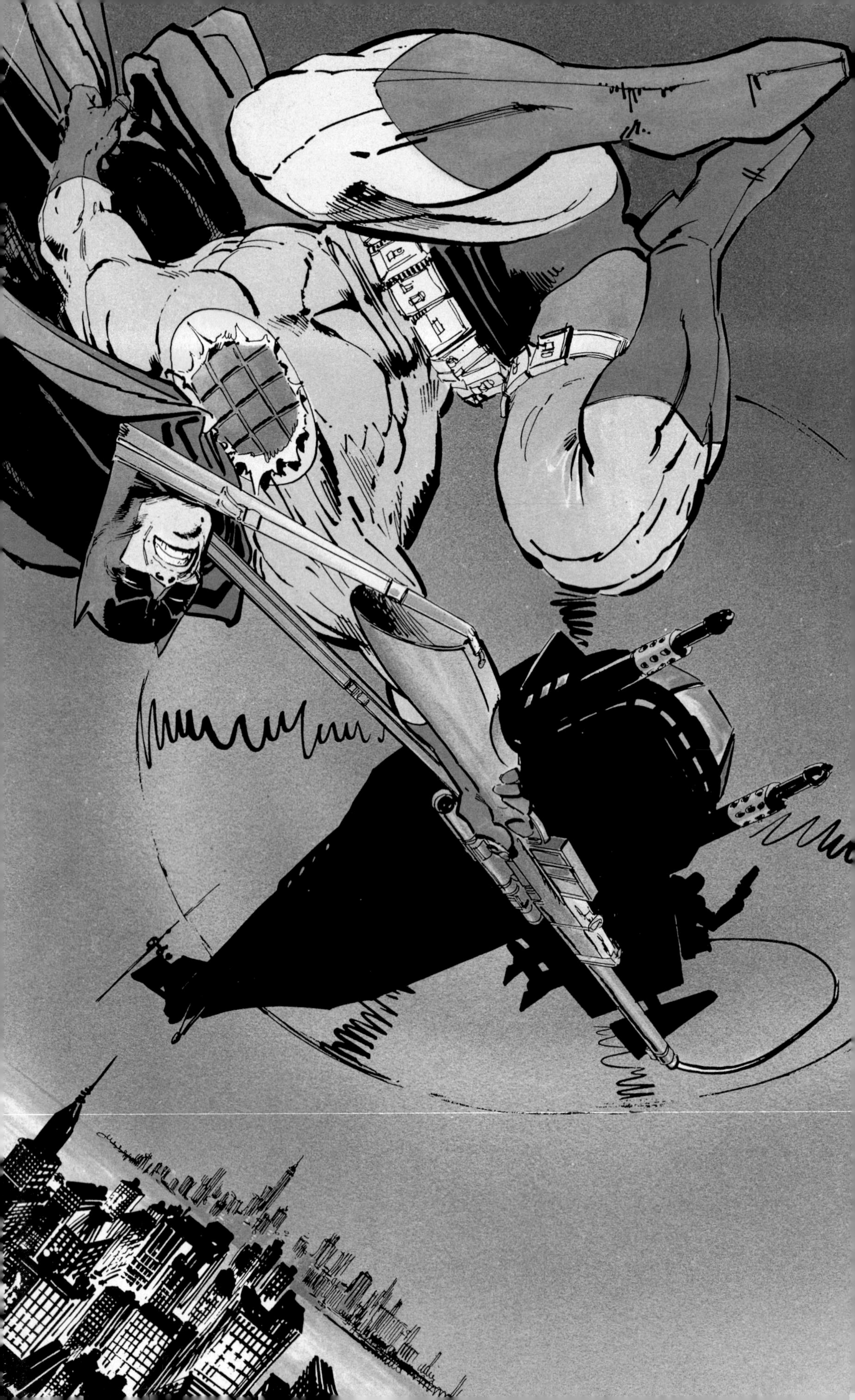

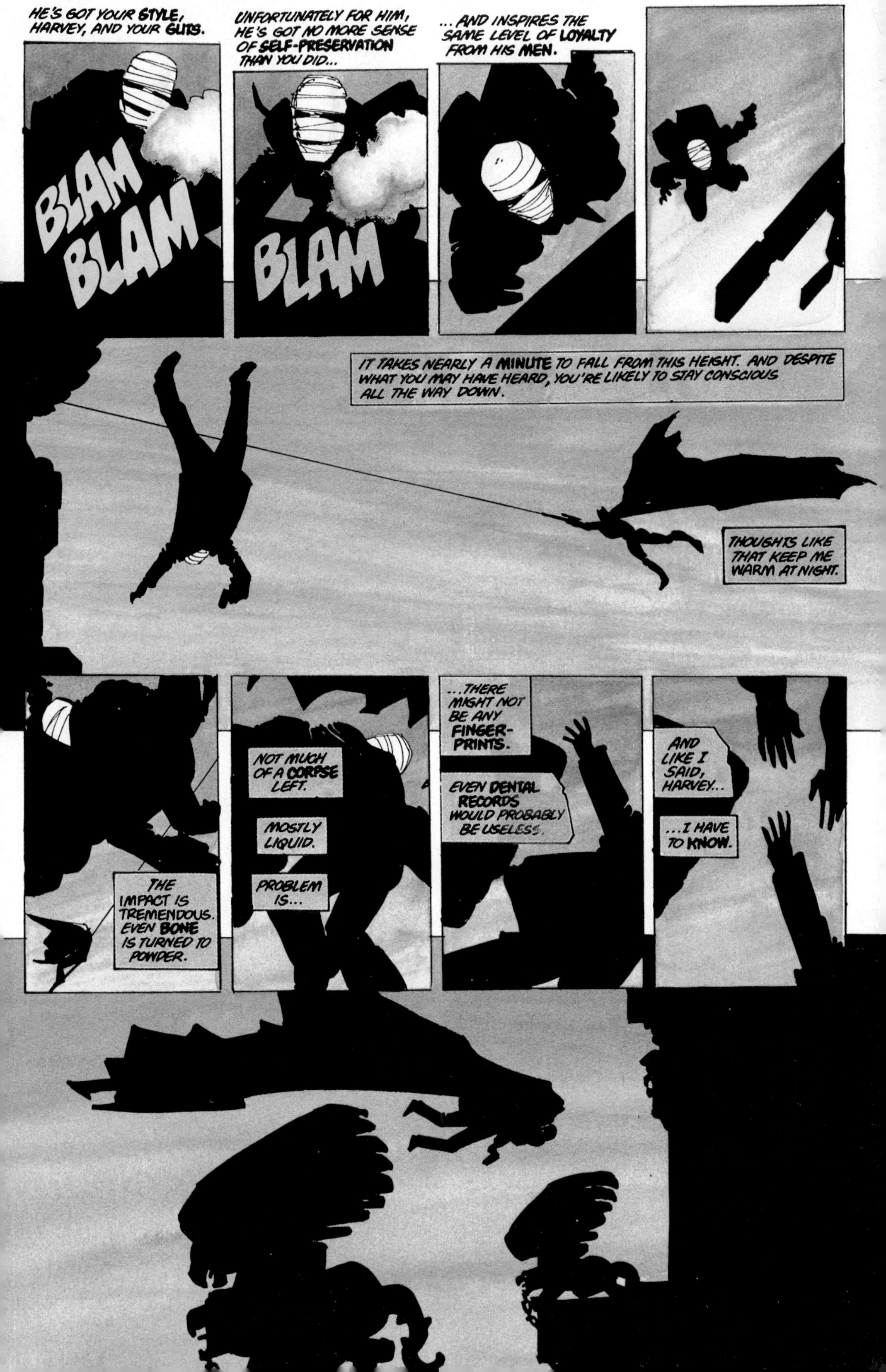
HE'S GOT YOUR STYLE, HARVEY, AND YOUR GUTS.
BLAM BLAM
UNFORTUNATELY FOR HIM, HE'S GOT NO MORE SENSE OF SELF-PRESERVATION THAN YOU DID...
BLAM
...AND INSPIRES THE SAME LEVEL OF LOYALTY FROM HIS MEN.
IT TAKES NEARLY A MINUTE TO FALL FROM THIS HEIGHT. AND DESPITE WHAT YOU MAY HAVE HEARD, YOU'RE LIKELY TO STAY CONSCIOUS ALL THE WAY DOWN.
THOUGHTS LIKE THAT KEEP ME WARM AT NIGHT.
THE IMPACT IS TREMENDOUS. EVEN BONE IS TURNED TO POWDER.
NOT MUCH OF A CORPSE LEFT.
MOSTLY LIQUID.
PROBLEM IS...
...THERE MIGHT NOT BE ANY FINGER-PRINTS.
EVEN DENTAL RECORDS WOULD PROBABLY BE USELESS.
AND LIKE I SAID, HARVEY...
...I HAVE TO KNOW.

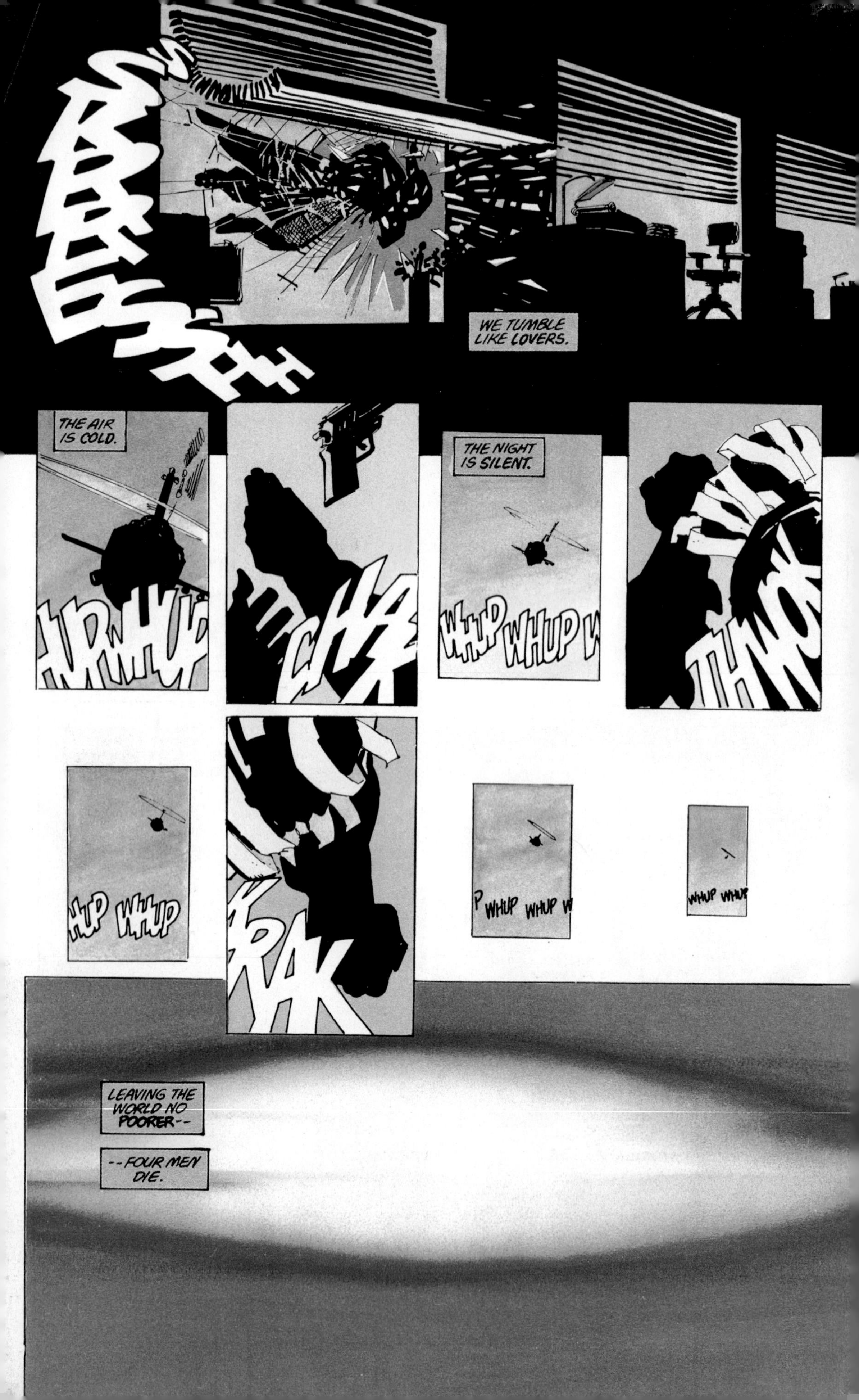
WE TUMBLE LIKE LOVERS.
THE AIR IS COLD.
THE NIGHT IS SILENT.
WHUP WHUP W
HUP WHUP
P WHUP WHUP W
WHUP WHUP
LEAVING THE WORLD NO POORER--
--FOUR MEN DIE.

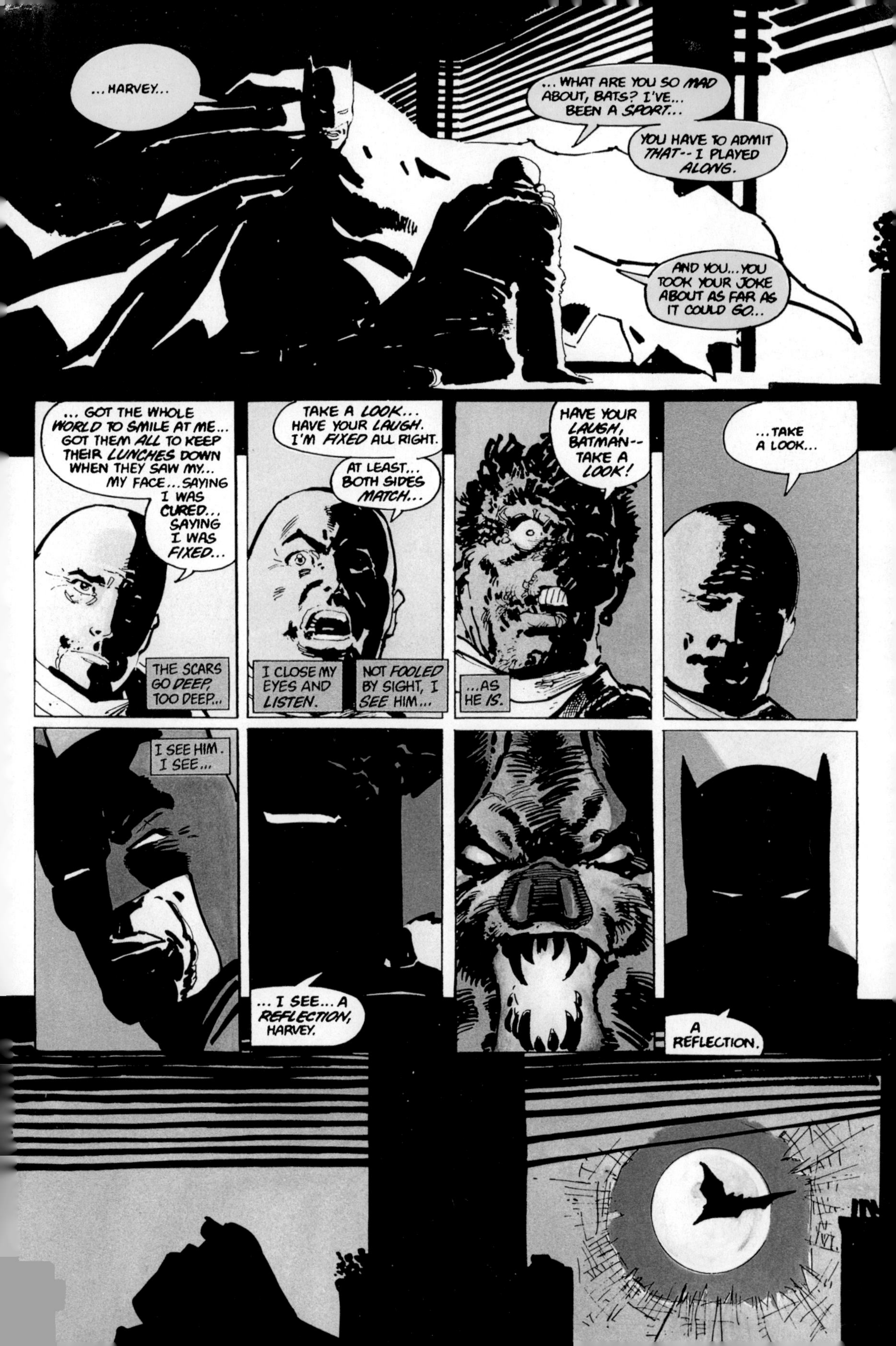

... HARVEY...
... WHAT ARE YOU SO MAD ABOUT, BATS? I'VE... BEEN A SPORT...
YOU HAVE TO ADMIT THAT-- I PLAYED ALONG.
AND YOU... YOU TOOK YOUR JOKE ABOUT AS FAR AS IT COULD GO...
... GOT THE WHOLE WORLD TO SMILE AT ME... GOT THEM ALL TO KEEP THEIR LUNCHES DOWN WHEN THEY SAW MY... MY FACE... SAYING I WAS CURED... SAYING I WAS FIXED...
THE SCARS GO DEEP, TOO DEEP...
TAKE A LOOK... HAVE YOUR LAUGH. I'M FIXED ALL RIGHT.
AT LEAST... BOTH SIDES MATCH...
I CLOSE MY EYES AND LISTEN.
NOT FOOLED BY SIGHT, I SEE HIM...
HAVE YOUR LAUGH, BATMAN-- TAKE A LOOK!
...AS HE IS.
...TAKE A LOOK...
I SEE HIM. I SEE...
... I SEE... A REFLECTION, HARVEY.
A REFLECTION.

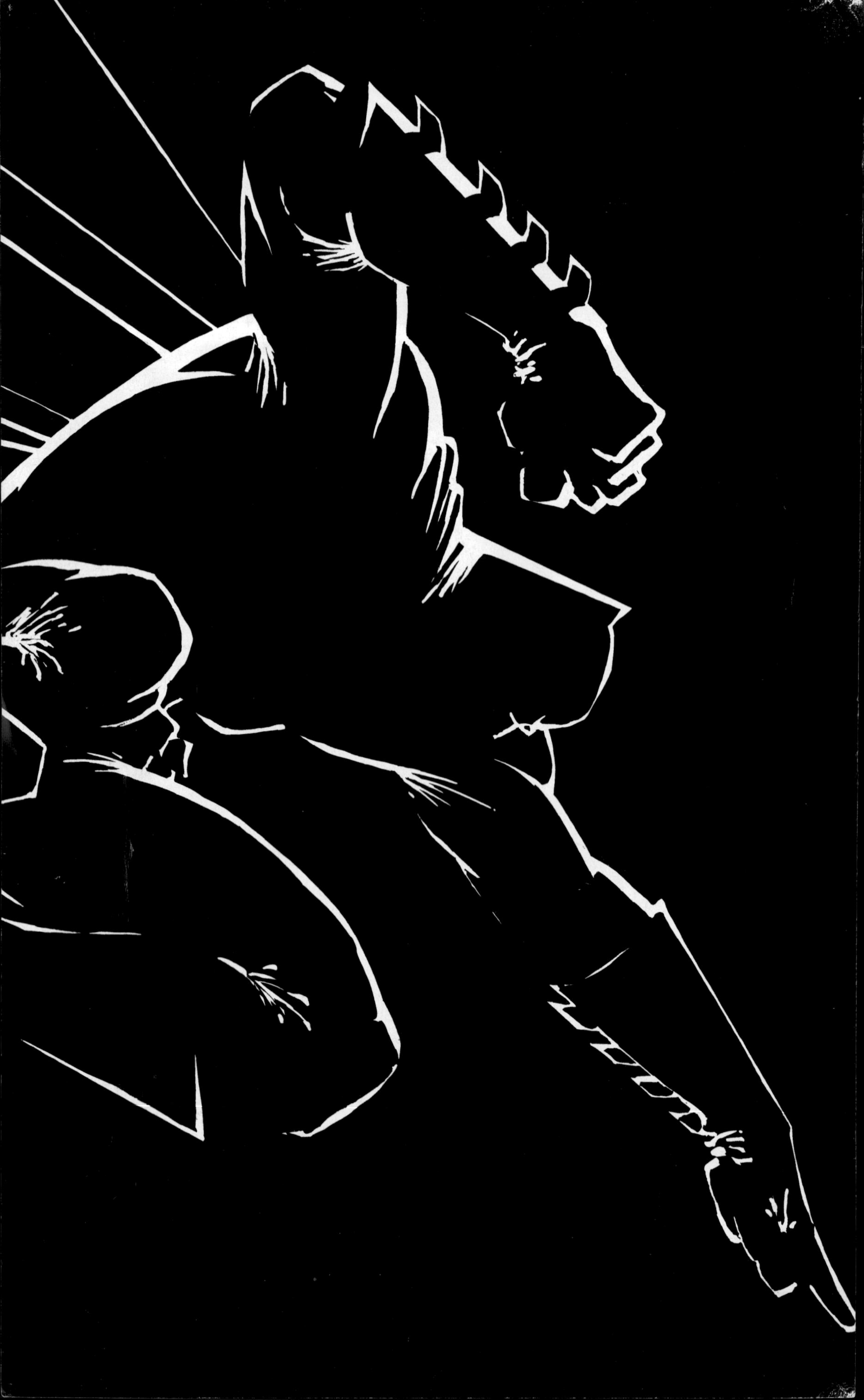